PASTA ET CETERA **à la di Stasio**

Gourmand World Cookbook Awards / French Canada **– Best TV Tie-In Cookbook**
Best Italian Cookbook – Best Cookbook Photography

PASTA ET CETERA **à la di Stasio**

Recipes by Josée di Stasio

Photography by Jean Longpré

Transcontinental Books
1100 René-Lévesque Boulevard West, 24th floor
Montreal, Quebec H3B 4X9
Tel.: 514-340-3587 / Toll-free 1-866-800-2500

Bibliothèque et Archives nationales du Québec and Library and Archives Canada cataloguing in publication
Di Stasio, Josée
    Pasta et cetera à la di Stasio
    Translation of: Pasta et cetera à la di Stasio.
    Includes index.
    Text in English only.
    ISBN 978-0-9809924-8-9
    1. Cookery (Pasta). 2. Cookery, Italian. I. Title.
TX809.M17D5213 2009   641.8'22   C2009-941709-X

Production coordinator **Marie-Suzanne Menier**
Translation **Michele Glazebrook**
Editing and proofreading **Christina Anson Mine**
Photos of Josée di Stasio, cover and pages 8 and 53 **© Monic Richard 2009**
Food stylist and consultant **Stéphan Boucher**
Copy and content editing **Josée Robitaille**
Assistant photographer (recipes) **Nathalie Chapdelaine**
Assistant photographer (cover and pages 8 and 53) **Maxime Desbiens**
Colour photo digitization **Shared Production Centre of Montreal, Transcontinental Media**
Page and cover design **orangetango**
Printed by Transcontinental Interglobe

This book was originally published in French under the same title
by Flammarion Québec and Josée di Stasio © 2007

Printed in Canada
© Transcontinental Books and Josée di Stasio, 2009 (English version published in Canada)
Legal deposit — 4th quarter 2009
National Library of Quebec
National Library of Canada

We acknowledge the financial support of the Government of Canada through
the Book Publishing Industry Development Program (BPIDP) and the Government
of Quebec through the SODEC Tax Credit for our publishing activities.

For information on special rates for corporate libraries and wholesale purchases, please call **1-866-800-2500.**

TABLE OF CONTENTS

FOR MY GRANDPARENTS – Upon leaving the Italian soil to make Montreal their home, my di Stasio grandparents brought with them the conviction that eating well was the guarantee of day-to-day happiness. Their modest means did not prevent my grandmother from cooking dishes that were always flavourful. In her kitchen were the essentials: a mixture of dried herbs given to her by the neighbour at summer's end, a bottle of olive oil, garlic, hot peppers and fresh ingredients. And her essentials are the basis of my palette of Mediterranean flavours. This book brings me closer to my Italian origins, and it was in thinking of my grandparents, Mariannina and Guido, that I wrote it. I'm certain they'd have been thrilled with the shows we shot in Italy—and with my progress in Italian.

ITALIAN COOKING MAKES YOU HAPPY – These pages capture Italy and its everyday, tasty, convivial and uncomplicated cuisine. Its simplicity promises the pleasure of remembering that there are seasons and local products, and of taking the time to savour them. I met many wonderful people in Italy and learned many cooking tips, but what I took away first and foremost is that all good cooking begins with good-quality ingredients, *punto*. Italians have enough faith in their products to not adulterate them, which, in itself, is a form of sophistication.

I admire the pride they take in passing on their culinary traditions. For an Italian, the right way to do something is the way it's done at home. Every family claims that its own recipe is the best. And each one is different! Italians don't just eat; they talk about eating—and have lots to say on the subject. Their enthusiasm makes you want to adopt these food lovers' heritage of flavours, aromas and a certain *dolce vita*. This is what I want to share with you through these recipes.

PASTA ET CETERA

This book is a guide, a repository of recipes that I've made my own and that are just waiting for your personal touch. The recipes come from all over: my reading, friends, family, travels and, of course, all the guests who have shared my dishes. While many of them closely adhere to tradition, some stray from conventions. May my Italian friends forgive me. Zucchini and feta pasta: what on earth? Can a limoncello made with vodka still be called by that name? Macaroni with Cheddar? Heavens! Everything is done by intuition rather than following the recipe down to the letter. I'm offering you my version. What will your version be?

Contrary to the custom of the Italians, who serve pasta as the *primo piatto* (first course), we eat it as our main course. You'll find colourful pasta dishes made with market produce, comfort food for the colder months, several vegetarian offerings, recipes sophisticated enough for company, and many dishes that require few ingredients and even less time to make. With more than 50 recipes and nearly as many variations, you can enjoy a different pasta dish every week for almost two years.

To accompany them, I've selected easy-to-make antipasti that can be savoured with a good glass of wine, and sweets to prolong the pleasure of conversation around the dinner table. At the back of the book, a section provides basic recipes and tips to simplify your time in the kitchen. A glossary presents the Italian products used in the recipes and suggests substitutes.

Often, the best recipes are the ones we improvise. Cooking by instinct is a pleasure. So don't hesitate to adjust the quantities as you see fit—and experiment. That's all there is to it. And you'll see that it often turns out even better that way.

ANTIPASTI & MINESTRE

COCKTAILS & APPETIZERS

Antipasti translates as "What comes before the meal."

You can either take pleasure in cooking these dishes or simply serve crudités, olives, cold meats and cheeses. And if you find a good prepared spread for bruschetta, why not? The trick is finding quality products that are in season or prepared by talented artisans.

If you feel like cooking, in this chapter I propose finger foods to nibble on with cocktails, along with some appetizers. Any one of them can be transformed into a pleasant lunch. Many of these recipes can be prepared in advance, because cocktail hour is the time to take part in *la dolce vita!* Let yourself be inspired by the images and guided by your taste buds.

CHEESE TUILES

People always fight over the fine, crispy crust of an *au gratin* dish. Well, there is plenty for everyone in this still-popular retro dish. Invariably, the plate will be cleaned.

MAKES 12 TUILES

2/3 cup (150 mL) grated grana Padano or Parmesan cheese

+ 2/3 cup (150 mL) shredded Cheddar cheese*

+ 2 tbsp (30 mL) sesame seeds or pistachios (see p. 173), ground (optional)

*These tuiles can also be prepared using only grana Padano or Parmesan.

Preheat oven to 350°F (180°C). Line a baking sheet with parchment paper or a silicone baking mat, or use a nonstick baking sheet.

…

In a bowl, mix grana Padano and cheddar cheeses.

…

Place 2 tbsp (30 mL) cheese mixture on baking sheet and flatten with a fork to make a tuile approximately 3 inches (8 cm) in diameter. Repeat, spacing tuiles at least 2 inches (5 cm) apart.

…

Top with sesame seeds or pistachios (if using).

…

Bake on middle rack of oven for about 10 minutes. Watch carefully, as the tuiles are ready when light golden (do not overcook, or the cheese will turn bitter). Remove from oven and wait a few minutes before touching the tuiles with a spatula. Let cool on a rack.

…

Tuiles will keep for a few days in a sealed cookie tin. As required, heat for 1 to 2 minutes in the oven to crisp them up.

SALAMI CHIPS

These are so fast and easy – munch on them with crudités and olives at cocktail hour or use as a garnish on salads or pasta.

MAKES 12 CHIPS

12 very thin slices salami

Preheat oven to 350°F (180°C).

…

Place salami on a baking sheet. Bake for 7 to 10 minutes, turning halfway through. Drain on paper towels.

…

Salami chips will keep for a few days in a sealed cookie tin. If chips will be eaten the same day, keep them at room temperature; if not, store in refrigerator. Immediately before serving, heat for 1 to 2 minutes in the oven to crisp them up.

LITTLE LEEK BALLS

It never fails – when there is a plate of these hors d'oeuvres with drinks,
every one of them disappears!

MAKES 30 TO 36 BALLS

3 tbsp (45 mL) olive oil or butter
+ 4 cups (1 L) diced leeks (white
  parts only)
+ 1 large egg
+ 1/2 cup (125 mL) crumbled or diced
  dry bread
+ 1/2 cup (125 mL) grated Parmesan
  cheese
+ Salt and freshly ground pepper

Preheat oven to 350°F (180°C).
...

In a large frying pan, heat 2 tbsp
(30 mL) of the oil over medium heat
and sauté diced leeks for 5 minutes,
taking care not to let them brown.
Cook for 5 to 10 more minutes.
...

In a bowl, beat egg and add bread,
Parmesan, remaining oil and
sautéed leeks. Season with salt and
pepper to taste. Mix well, ideally in a
food processor.
...

Shape into 1-inch (2.5 cm) balls,
pressing firmly. Place on lightly
greased baking sheet.
...

Bake for 20 minutes, turning once,
until golden.
...

Serve hot or warm at cocktail hour,
with crudités and olives.

ARUGULA SHOOTERS

To ensure maximum enjoyment, chill the small glasses in the freezer.
My recipe is inspired by Heinz Beck, a restaurateur at the Hilton Hotel in Rome.

MAKES 8 TO 10 SHOOTERS

2 cups (500 mL) arugula, stems removed
+ 2 cups (500 mL) lemon sorbet*
+ 1 cup (250 mL) ginger ale
+ Vodka (optional)

*Choose a good-quality sorbet that's not too
sweet and doesn't contain any dairy products.

Place shooter glasses in freezer at
least 30 minutes before using.
...

In blender, purée arugula, sorbet,
ginger ale, and vodka (if using) until
blended.
...

Pour into frosted glasses and serve
immediately.

SAUSAGE BITES

This beautiful recipe comes from the handsome Stefano Faita.
Nibble these bites with drinks, or enjoy them in a sandwich or with tomato sauce.

MAKES 48 TO 60 BITES

About 2 cups (500 mL) fresh bread crumbs (crusts removed)
+ 3/4 cup (175 mL) milk
+ 1/2 lb (250 g) Italian sausages
+ 1/2 lb (250 g) ground veal
+ 1 cup (250 mL) grated Parmesan cheese
+ 1/4 cup (50 mL) Italian flat-leaf parsley, chopped
+ 1 tsp (5 mL) grated nutmeg
+ 1 large egg
+ Salt and freshly ground pepper
+ A little oil and/or butter

Preheat oven to 375°F (190°C).

...

In a large bowl, soak bread crumbs in milk for 15 minutes.

...

Remove casings from sausages. Add sausage meat to bread mixture along with veal, Parmesan, parsley, nutmeg and egg. Season with salt and pepper to taste and mix well. If consistency is too soft, add more bread crumbs, soaking them in milk if you like.

...

Shape into 1-inch (2.5 cm) balls.

...

In a frying pan, heat oil over medium-high heat and fry meatballs, turning often, for 7 minutes or until evenly browned, about .

...

Place meatballs on baking sheet. Bake in oven for 10 to 15 minutes or until meatballs are no longer pink in centre.

...

Serve with drinks or for lunch alongside a salad and a few tomato quarters.

SERVING SUGGESTIONS

With pasta: Add meatballs to tomato sauce and pour over pasta.

...

In a sandwich: Shape mixture into patties, cook and serve in a sandwich.

RED PEPPER DIP

This full-flavoured dip goes with just about everything.

MAKES 1 1/4 CUPS (300 ML)

2 or 3 red peppers, roasted and peeled (see p. 176), or jarred roasted red peppers, drained, rinsed and dried

+ 1/2 cup (125 mL) blanched almonds or lightly toasted pine nuts (see p. 173)

+ 2 cloves garlic, roasted (see p. 170), or a pinch of chopped garlic

+ Large handful fresh basil or another favourite herb

+ Hot pepper sauce, such as Tabasco, or cayenne pepper, to taste

+ Salt

+ 3 to 4 tbsp (45 to 60 mL) olive oil

+ 1 tbsp (15 mL) balsamic or red wine vinegar

Place peppers, almonds, garlic, basil and hot pepper sauce in blender. Season with salt to taste and purée until smooth.

…

Gradually add oil and blend to a mayonnaise-like consistency. Blend in vinegar. Adjust seasoning.

TO SERVE

Serve with a platter of crudités, including sliced fennel, cucumber and celery.

…

Spread on crostini and garnish with diced pitted black olives.

…

Serve as an appetizer with grilled shrimp.

…

Serve alongside fish or grilled meats.

…

Serve with slices of fresh mozzarella drizzled with olive oil and sprinkled with pepper.

ANTIPASTI & MINESTRE – 19

BRUSCHETTA AND CROSTINI

BRUSCHETTA These slices of country-style or rustic bread, left whole or cut in half, are ideally toasted over a wood fire or on the barbecue. If not, they can be broiled in the oven or simply popped into the toaster. The bread is sometimes rubbed with a halved garlic clove while still hot. Toasting helps the bread absorb more garlic flavour. Since bruschetta are often drizzled with olive oil, take the opportunity to use a good-quality one. And if you want to add salt, opt for sea salt. Bruschetta are served with antipasti, as an appetizer or for lunch. In Italy, the tradition is to sample freshly pressed oil by drizzling it onto these toasts. CROSTINI Similar to croûtes, crostini are smaller than bruschetta and made with thin slices of baguette or *ficelle* loaf, or even a slice of bread cut into quarters. The bread is baked on a baking sheet in the oven at 350°F (180°C) for 10 to 15 minutes or until golden. Once again, the hot bread can be rubbed with a halved garlic clove, or brushed with oil before or after baking.

————————

SWEET PEPPER COMPOTE

Take full advantage of pepper season by mixing hot and mild varieties in this compote. In addition to serving it with cocktails, you can add some to pasta or bean salads— in other words, you'll be glad if you have any left over!

MAKES 3 CUPS (750 ML)

1/4 cup (50 mL) olive oil

+ 5 sweet red, yellow or orange peppers, peel optional, diced
+ Hot pepper (finely chopped fresh hot pepper, hot pepper flakes or hot pepper paste), to taste
+ 1 onion, chopped
+ Salt and freshly ground pepper
+ 1 or 2 cloves garlic, chopped (optional)
+ 1/2 cup (125 mL) mixed pitted black and green olives, chopped (optional)
+ 1/4 cup (50 mL) snipped fresh mint or other herb of your choice
+ 2 to 3 tbsp (30 to 45 mL) capers

*If you peel the peppers (see p. 176), reduce the cooking time.

In a large skillet, heat oil over medium-high heat and sauté sweet and hot peppers and onion for 20 minutes, stirring often. Season with salt and pepper to taste. Add garlic and cook for 1 minute more.

...

Remove from heat and add olives (if using), mint and capers. Season to taste with salt and pepper.

TO SERVE

Serve compote on bruschetta or chunks of baked pizza dough. You'll find pre-oiled, pre-seasoned pizza crusts at the grocery store.

SERVING SUGGESTIONS

With goat cheese: Spread soft goat cheese onto toasts and spoon Sweet Pepper Compote over top.

...

With poultry or meat: Serve as a condiment for cold roast chicken or grilled white meat (pork or veal).

...

On sandwiches: Use as a topping for burgers and panini.

NOTE

Sweet Pepper Compote tastes even better the day after it's made. Add capers and olives just before serving.

ANCHOVY CHEESE SPREAD

I discovered this subtly flavoured dip at the home of Evelina, my Italian teacher. It contains only two ingredients, and it's delicious. Keep a tube of anchovy paste in the fridge and you can improvise vinaigrettes, sauces, mayonnaise, pasta and *ancora di più.*

MAKES 1/2 CUP (125 ML)
4 oz (125 g) room-temperature cream cheese or mascarpone
+ 1 tbsp (15 mL) anchovy paste
+ Garnish (optional): freshly ground pepper, chopped fresh chives or lemon zest

In a bowl, blend cheese and anchovy paste well.

TO SERVE
Spread mixture on crostini, cucumber slices, chunks of fennel, endive spears or celery stalks. Top with garnish (if using). This spread is also good as a dip with grissini (Italian breadsticks).

ROSEMARY WHITE BEAN SPREAD

This purée is delicious on bread rubbed with garlic. Delightful with cocktails, it's always a pleasure at lunch, too, in sandwiches or with raw vegetable sticks.

MAKES 2 CUPS (500 ML)
3 tbsp (45 mL) olive oil
+ 1 onion, chopped
+ 2 cloves garlic, chopped
+ 1 can (19 oz/540 mL) cannellini or other white beans, drained and rinsed
+ Juice of 1 lemon
+ 1 to 2 tbsp (15 to 30 mL) chopped fresh rosemary or 3 tbsp (45 mL) finely chopped fresh basil
+ Salt and freshly ground pepper
+ Garnish (optional): grated lemon rind or olive oil

In a skillet, heat oil over medium-low heat and sauté onion until translucent. Add garlic for the last minute of cooking. Transfer mixture to food processor.
···

Add beans, lemon juice and rosemary. Season with salt and pepper to taste. Purée. If the spread is too thick, add a little water or more lemon juice.

TO SERVE
Garnish with grated lemon rind or drizzle with olive oil (if using).

ARTICHOKE SPREAD

This unbelievably simple spread is a guaranteed hit for cocktail nibbles. The ingredients are all easy to keep on hand.

MAKES 3/4 CUP (175 ML)
1 cup (250 mL) marinated artichoke hearts, drained
+ 5 tbsp (75 mL) grated Parmesan cheese
+ 1 tsp (5 mL) finely grated lemon rind
+ Olive oil or lemon-flavoured olive oil, to taste
+ Salt and freshly ground pepper
+ Chopped Italian flat-leaf parsley (optional)
+ Chopped black or stuffed green olives (optional)

Reserving a few artichokes, place artichokes, Parmesan cheese and lemon rind in food processor. Process, adding the oil in a thin stream, until almost smooth. Transfer to a bowl.
···

Chop reserved artichokes and stir into purée. Season with salt and pepper to taste. Add parsley and olives (if using).

NOTE
This spread can be made ahead of time to allow the flavours to develop.

PROSCIUTTO

A good cured ham is simplicity itself.
Have it thinly sliced by the butcher and eat it as soon as possible.
WITH FRUIT Traditionally, prosciutto is served with melon. Choose a good one – it should be heavy,
pleasantly scented and bruise-free. Season generously with pepper and voilà!
Or try it with fresh or grilled figs. It's also delicious with pears or peaches. WITH CHEESE Serve
prosciutto with mozzarella, a drizzle of good olive oil and freshly ground pepper.
Or try it with a chunk of Parmesan or grana Padano cheese.
WITH BREAD Serve alongside grissini, or crusty country-style bread spread
with unsalted butter or drizzled with oil. WITH SALAD Pair with arugula, baby greens or chicory,
shaved Parmesan and pear quarters.

PROSCIUTTO AND ASPARAGUS WITH MUSTARD SAUCE

I prefer thick, fleshy asparagus spears for this twist on a traditional recipe.
It makes great finger food, but it can be served as a first course as well.

MAKES 32 PIECES

1/2 cup (125 mL) crème fraîche*
+ 2 tbsp (30 mL) old-fashioned mustard (grainy or stone-ground)
+ Grated rind of 1 lemon (organic if possible)
+ Salt and freshly ground pepper
+ 16 thick asparagus spears, trimmed (see p. 170)
+ 8 thin slices prosciutto

*If you prefer, you can substitute cream cheese (beat with a little milk or cream to thin), or plain yogurt, drained for 1 hour in a sieve lined with cheesecloth or paper towel.

In a bowl, mix cream, mustard and lemon rind. Season with salt and pepper to taste. Set aside.

⋯

In a pot of boiling salted water, cook asparagus for 2 to 3 minutes or until tender-crisp. Plunge immediately into ice water to stop cooking. Drain and cut spears in half.

⋯

Cut each slice of prosciutto into 4 pieces. Roll 1 around each half-spear.

⋯

Arrange on platter. Serve with mustard sauce on the side.

NOTE

To serve these prosciutto rolls as an appetizer, arrange on plates and drizzle sauce over each portion.

BRESAOLA AND GOAT CHEESE BITES

To learn more about bresaola, take a look at the glossary at the end of this book (see p. 184).
This salty cured meat is delicious with melon, figs and pears.

MAKES 18 PIECES

5 oz (150 g) creamy goat cheese
+ 2 tsp (10 mL) grated lemon rind
+ Olive oil
+ Salt and freshly ground pepper
+ 18 thin slices bresaola or air-dried Grisons beef
+ 18 leaves arugula or watercress, stems removed

In a bowl, mix cheese, lemon rind and enough oil to make a creamy mixture. Season with salt and pepper to taste.

...

Spread a little of the cheese mixture on one-half of each slice of bresaola. Top with arugula and fold over into a sandwich.

...

Serve with drinks.

BRESAOLA WITH PINK GRAPEFRUIT

I first experienced this marriage of air-dried Grisons beef and grapefruit in Switzerland.
I rediscovered the same twosome in Italy, made with bresaola (see p. 184), and I must say,
they definitely make a harmonious couple.

1 pink grapefruit
+ 12 to 16 thin slices bresaola or air-dried Grisons beef
+ A drizzle of olive oil or lemon-flavoured olive oil
+ Freshly ground pepper
+ A handful of small arugula or watercress leaves

Peel grapefruit, removing pith. Divide into segments (see p. 170).

...

On a large plate, arrange bresaola slices. Places grapefruit segments in centre.

JUST BEFORE SERVING

Drizzle with oil and season generously with pepper to taste. Garnish with arugula and serve.

PIZZA SCAPPATA

Scappata means "escaped," like the crust on this pizza. This recipe is a childhood memory that Giampaolo Motta shared with us on an episode of the show that we shot in the Chianti area of Tuscany in Italy. This dish is the essence of conviviality!

SERVES 4

2 to 3 tbsp (30 to 45 mL) olive oil
+ 1 clove garlic, cut in half
+ 1 can (19 oz/540 mL) whole or diced tomatoes
+ Salt
+ 1 ball mozzarella di bufala or mozzarina, or 4 bocconcini
+ A handful of fresh basil leaves, torn
+ A drizzle of olive oil
+ Freshly ground pepper (optional)
+ Country-style bread

In a large skillet, heat oil over low heat and infuse garlic for 3 to 4 minutes without browning.

…

Add tomatoes and season with salt to taste. Cook over medium-high heat, stirring often, for about 10 minutes. Lightly mash tomatoes with a fork. Continue cooking for a few more minutes to reduce sauce. Remove garlic.

…

Slice cheese and place on top of sauce. Let melt, without stirring, for 1 minute. Remove from heat.

…

Sprinkle with basil and drizzle with olive oil. Season with pepper to taste (if using).

TO SERVE

Savour pizza scappata straight from the pan, dipping bread into it.

CLAM BRUSCHETTA

Make this tasty dish with clams or mussels – it's your choice. What makes a difference is the freshness of the shellfish – the fresher, the better. Serve with good toasted bread to soak up the cooking juices.

SERVES 4

2 lb (1 kg) small fresh clams*
+ 3 tbsp (45 mL) olive oil
+ 2 cloves garlic, cut in half
+ 2 shallots or 1 small onion, finely diced
+ 3/4 cup (175 mL) white wine
+ Hot pepper flakes, to taste (optional)
+ 1/2 cup (125 mL) chopped Italian
  flat-leaf parsley
+ 4 slices country-style bread
+ A drizzle of olive oil
+ Freshly ground pepper

*You can also make this dish with mussels if desired. Just increase the quantity.

Wash clams in cold water, scrubbing well.

…

In a large pot, heat oil over low heat and fry 3 half-cloves of the garlic with shallots, stirring, for 4 to 5 minutes or until golden.

…

Add white wine and hot pepper flakes (if using) and bring to a boil.

…

Add clams. Reduce heat to medium-high, cover and cook, stirring occasionally, for 7 to 8 minutes or until shells open. Discard any clams that do not open.

…

Add parsley and mix well.

…

Toast bread slices and rub with remaining half-clove garlic. Place 1 slice in each of 4 deep soup plates. Arrange clams on bread and pour a spoonful of cooking juices over top, taking care to leave any grit from the clams in the bottom of the pot.

…

Drizzle with olive oil, season with pepper to taste and serve immediately.

SALADS

Italian salads are very simple to make – no fussy dressings emulsified with mustard and, most importantly, a short list of ingredients. Some wine or balsamic vinegar, salt, a lovingly selected high-quality olive oil and freshly ground pepper – nothing more. Season at the last minute and toss salad gently to avoid bruising the leaves. Lemon juice can replace the vinegar, or you can mix the two. For extra flavour, add: garlic to taste, rubbed onto the bowl or mashed with a little salt; anchovies crushed with a fork into the vinegar or lemon juice; grated or shaved Parmesan or grana Padano cheese; or a handful of fresh herbs.

––––––––

SICILIAN ORANGE SALAD

My paternal grandmother used to prepare this salad, to our great delight.
This recipe illustrates the simplicity of Italian cuisine.

SERVES 6

1 medium red onion
+ 4 oranges, peeled and pith removed
+ A drizzle of olive oil
+ Salt and freshly ground pepper
+ Black olives (optional)

Peel and thinly slice onion. Soak in cold water for 10 minutes. Drain and pat dry.

…

Cut oranges into 1/4-inch (5 mm) thick slices.

…

Place orange slices on serving platter. Top with onion slices. Drizzle with oil and season with salt and pepper to taste.

TO SERVE
Garnish with olives (if using). Serve cold.

SERVING SUGGESTION
Top with thinly sliced fennel.

ASPARAGUS SALAD WITH SOFT-BOILED EGGS

Make this again and again when asparagus is in season. As an appetizer, or for lunch with crusty bread, this salad is generous and exquisite.

SERVES 4

4 thin slices pancetta or bacon (optional)
+ 16 medium asparagus spears, trimmed (see p. 170)
+ 1 tbsp (15 mL) balsamic or red wine vinegar
+ Salt and freshly ground pepper
+ 3 tbsp (45 mL) olive oil
+ 4 large eggs, at room temperature
+ Sliced Parmesan, grana Padano or Cheddar cheese

If using pancetta, preheat oven to 350°F (180°C). Place pancetta slices on baking sheet. Bake for 10 minutes or until crisp. Set aside.

...

In a pot of boiling salted water, cook asparagus for 2 to 3 minutes or until tender-crisp. Plunge immediately into ice water to stop cooking. Drain and set aside.

...

In a large bowl, whisk vinegar and salt and pepper to taste. Whisk in oil.

...

Cut asparagus into pieces and add to dressing. Toss to coat.

...

In a small pot of boiling water, cook eggs for 4 minutes or until soft-boiled*. Run under cold water to stop cooking. Peel.

*If you have mastered the art of poaching eggs, the salad is just as delicious with them.

TO SERVE

Arrange a portion of asparagus salad on each of 4 plates. Top with 1 of the eggs and garnish with cheese. Season with pepper to taste and garnish with 1 slice of the pancetta (if using).

...

SERVING SUGGESTION

The asparagus spears can be roasted (see p. 170) instead of boiled.

...

VARIATION

Green Bean Salad with Soft-Boiled Eggs: Replace asparagus with thin green beans.

MOZZARELLA

If you're lucky enough to get ahold of some lovely freshly made mozzarella di bufala, you don't need to add anything, except perhaps a drizzle of oil. This type of mozzarella has become popular thanks to the Caprese (tomato and basil) salad. This extremely simple dish can be endlessly transformed by using any of the multitude of tomatoes available today – they come in all colours and are full of flavour. A drizzle of oil, a different herb, and it's done. To fully enjoy mozzarella, Italians advise bringing it to room temperature before eating. Or soak it in warm water for a few minutes to soften.

ROASTED PEPPER SALAD
WITH SALSA VERDE

Enjoy this palette of colours and flavours on your plate. Use any leftover salsa verde on pasta, fish, grilled meats or vegetables.

SERVES 4

2 slices day-old bread, crusts removed, cubed*

+ 1 tbsp (15 mL) wine vinegar or lemon juice
+ 2 cups (500 mL) fresh herbs (such as Italian flat-leaf parsley, basil or mint) or arugula
+ 1 tbsp (15 mL) capers, drained and rinsed
+ 2 cloves Roasted Garlic (see p. 170) or a pinch of minced garlic
+ 4 anchovy fillets, rinsed and patted dry (optional)
+ About 1/2 cup (125 mL) olive oil
+ Salt and freshly ground pepper
+ 2 sweet yellow, orange or red peppers, roasted and peeled (see p. 176)
+ 1 ball mozzarella di bufala or 4 bocconcini, sliced
+ A few black olives

*You can omit the bread, but it does give the sauce a nice consistency. If omitting bread, add vinegar to the herb mixture before pulsing.

Place bread and vinegar in food processor and let stand for 2 minutes.

...

Add herbs, capers, garlic, and anchovies (if using). Pulse until well chopped. Pulse again, pouring in oil until blended but not too smooth. Season salsa verde with salt and pepper to taste. Set aside.

...

Quarter peppers and arrange on plate. Garnish with cheese, olives and a generous spoonful of the salsa verde. Season with more pepper if desired.

NOTE

You can make the salsa verde by hand using a chef's knife or mezzaluna, omitting bread. Prepare a few hours in advance. It will keep for several days in the refrigerator.

MARKET-FRESH CARPACCIO

The term *carpaccio*, traditionally reserved for beef, is now applied to thinly sliced raw vegetables, fruit and fish. This fresh, crisp salad is perfect before pasta. Its interest lies in the thinness of the vegetable slices. Here's your chance to use your good olive oil and fine salts.

SERVES 4

1 fennel bulb, halved lengthwise
(see p. 173)

+ 6 radishes
+ 2 small cucumbers
+ 1 stalk celery
+ 10 black olives, pitted and finely chopped
+ 1/4 cup (50 mL) olive oil or lemon-flavoured olive oil
+ 2 tbsp (30 mL) lemon or lime juice
+ Salt and freshly ground pepper
+ A drizzle of olive oil
+ Pecorino Romano or Parmesan cheese shards

Using a mandoline*, thinly slice fennel, radishes and cucumbers. Thinly slice celery on the diagonal.

...

Decoratively arrange vegetables on a platter or individual plates.

...

In a small bowl, mix olives, oil and lemon juice. Drizzle over vegetables. Season with salt and pepper to taste. Drizzle with olive oil and garnish with cheese shards.

*Handle the razor-sharp mandoline with care, using the finger guard to avoid injury.

SERVING SUGGESTION
Serve with sliced prosciutto, soppressata or sausage.

PARMESAN-CRUSTED PORTOBELLOS

This recipe was suggested to us while we were filming at the Modena market by Signora Maria, who had an impressive mushroom stall there.
The double Parmesan coating seals in the mushroom flavour.

SERVES 4

2 large or 4 small portobello mushrooms
+ 1/4 cup (50 mL) all-purpose flour
+ Salt and freshly ground pepper
+ 2 large eggs
+ 1/2 cup (125 mL) grated Parmesan cheese
+ 1/2 cup (125 mL) dry bread crumbs
+ 5 to 6 tbsp (75 to 90 mL) olive oil
+ Juice of 1/2 lemon
+ 6 cups (1.5 L) arugula, watercress, baby spinach, torn radicchio or mixed greens
+ Garnishes, to taste: snipped fine herbs, lemon wedges, pine nuts or other toasted nuts

Preheat oven to 350°F (180°C).

...

Brush or wipe mushrooms clean with a paper towel. Using a sharp knife, take a thin slice off the top of each mushroom to create a flat surface.

...

On a plate, season flour with salt and pepper to taste. In a small bowl, beat eggs with a fork and season with salt. On another plate, mix Parmesan and bread crumbs.

...

Dredge mushrooms in flour, shaking off excess. Dip into eggs, letting excess drip back into bowl. Coat mushrooms with bread crumb mixture, pressing lightly to coat well. Dip mushrooms into eggs then bread crumb mixture again.

...

In an ovenproof* nonstick skillet, heat about 2 tbsp (30 mL) of the oil over medium heat and brown mushrooms on both sides, adding more of the remaining oil as needed. Transfer mushrooms to baking sheet and bake in oven for about 15 minutes.

...

In a small bowl, whisk lemon juice and remaining oil. Toss with arugula. Season with salt and pepper to taste.

*To ovenproof a skillet, wrap aluminum foil around handle.

TO SERVE

Divide salad among individual plates. Cut up mushrooms and arrange over salad. Add desired garnishes and serve immediately.

NOTE

Mushrooms can be cooked ahead of time and reheated in the oven for a few minutes before serving.

SERVING SUGGESTIONS

Add a little walnut or pine nut oil to the olive oil in the salad.

...

Replace lemon juice with balsamic or other vinegar.

SOUPS

To me, whether serving *minestra in brodo* (a good stock with small pasta or vegetables) or a copious *zuppa* poured over a slice of bread in the bowl, soup is always synonymous with comfort.

––––––––

TORTELLINI IN BRODO

Combine a good, well-flavoured stock with tasty tortellini...it's magic! For extra zip, you can add vegetables or a handful of fine herbs. This simple soup is a balm to the senses.

SERVES 4

8 to 12 oz (250 to 375 g) fresh or frozen tortellini

+ 6 cups (1.5 L) good-quality canned or homemade chicken stock (see p. 172)
+ A handful of baby spinach, chopped Italian flat-leaf parsley or watercress leaves
+ Salt and freshly ground pepper
+ Grated Parmesan cheese

In a large pot of boiling salted water, cook tortellini until al dente. Drain.
…
Pour stock into pot. Add tortellini and spinach. Bring to a boil and cook for 1 minute or until spinach is just wilted. Season with salt and pepper to taste.

JUST BEFORE SERVING
Sprinkle with Parmesan cheese.

TORTELLINI AND TOMATO BOUILLON

SERVES 4

8 to 12 oz (250 to 375 g) fresh or frozen tortellini

+ 1 tbsp (15 mL) olive oil
+ 1 onion, minced
+ 6 cups (1.5 L) good-quality canned or homemade chicken stock (see p. 172)
+ 2 tbsp (30 mL) tomato paste
+ A generous pinch of saffron (optional)
+ Salt and freshly ground pepper
+ Grated Parmesan cheese

In a large pot of boiling salted water, cook tortellini until al dente. Drain.
…
In a soup pot, heat oil over medium-high heat and fry onion until golden.
…
Pour in stock. Stir in tomato paste, and saffron (if using). Add tortellini and heat through. Season with salt and pepper to taste.

JUST BEFORE SERVING
Sprinkle with Parmesan cheese.

TORTELLINI AND MUSHROOM BOUILLON

SERVES 4

6 cups (1.5 L) good-quality canned or homemade chicken stock (see p. 172)

+ 1/2 oz (15 g) dried porcini mushrooms
+ 1 clove garlic, crushed
+ 8 to 12 oz (250 to 375 g) fresh or frozen tortellini
+ Salt and freshly ground pepper
+ Grated Parmesan cheese

In a large pot, bring stock, porcini mushrooms and garlic to a boil. Simmer, uncovered, for 15 to 20 minutes. Strain and set stock aside. Chop mushrooms.
…
Meanwhile, in a large pot of boiling salted water, cook tortellini until al dente. Drain.
…
Add tortellini and mushrooms to stock. Season with salt and pepper to taste.

JUST BEFORE SERVING
Sprinkle with Parmesan cheese.

BRODO CON POLPETTINE

In Italian, *brodo* means "broth" and *polpettine* means "little meatballs." This soup is often served as an appetizer for a holiday meal. It's also comforting as a meal the day after the party.

**SERVES 8 AS AN APPETIZER OR
4 AS A MEAL**

1 lb (500 g) ground veal
+ 1/2 cup (125 mL) dry bread crumbs
+ 1/4 cup (50 mL) grated Parmesan
  cheese
+ 1/4 cup (50 mL) chopped Italian
  flat-leaf parsley
+ 2 large eggs
+ Salt and freshly ground pepper
+ 8 cups (2 L) chicken stock
+ 2 small carrots, julienned (optional)
+ 2 handfuls chiffonade of baby spinach
  or escarole
+ Grated Parmesan cheese

In a bowl, mix veal, bread crumbs, Parmesan, parsley and eggs. Season with salt and pepper to taste and mix well. Fry a small amount of meat, taste and adjust seasoning if necessary.

...

Shape meat into 1-inch (2.5 cm) meatballs.

...

In a large pot, bring stock to a boil and add meatballs. Reduce heat to medium and simmer gently for 15 minutes without allowing broth to boil. Remove meatballs and keep warm.

...

For a clear broth (which is not obligatory), strain through a sieve lined with paper towel or cheesecloth.

...

Add carrots (if using) to broth and cook for 3 minutes. Add spinach and continue cooking until vegetables are tender. Return meatballs to broth and adjust seasoning.

...

Serve soup steaming hot, sprinkled with Parmesan cheese.

SERVING SUGGESTION

With small pasta: Before serving, add cooked pasta, such as stelline (little stars), mini tubetti, peperini or orzo.

NOTE

The *polpettine* can be frozen separately.

FISH SOUP WITH ORANGE AND FENNEL

This soup is served as a main course following a pasta appetizer or in small portions before pasta. The advantage of this soup is that it can be prepared in advance, without the fish, and frozen. Before serving, just gently poach your favourite fish in the soup.

SERVES 6

1 tbsp (15 mL) crushed fennel seeds

+ 1 tbsp (15 mL) grated orange rind

+ 3 tbsp (45 mL) olive oil

+ Salt and freshly ground pepper

+ 2 lb (1 kg) firm-fleshed fish (such as monkfish, halibut, cod or tilapia), cut in large chunks

+ 1 large or 2 medium fennel bulbs, minced

+ 1 large onion, minced

+ 1 leek, minced

+ 2 cloves garlic, crushed

+ 3 cups (750 mL) fish stock, clam juice or chicken stock

+ 1/2 cup (125 mL) white wine, or Noilly Prat or other dry vermouth (optional)

+ 1 can (28 oz/796 mL) diced tomatoes

+ 2 or 3 strips orange rind

+ 2 pinches of saffron

+ Shrimp, scallops or other shellfish (optional)

In a bowl, mix 1 tsp (5 mL) of the fennel seeds, the grated orange rind and 1 tbsp (15 mL) of the oil. Season with salt and pepper to taste. Coat fish with this seasoning and refrigerate for about 1 hour.

...

In a large soup pot, heat remaining oil over medium heat and fry minced fennel, onion and leek, stirring frequently, for 5 minutes. Add garlic and cook for 1 minute more.

...

Add fish stock, wine (if using), tomatoes, remaining fennel seeds, orange rind strips and saffron. Season with salt and pepper to taste. Bring to a boil; reduce heat to low and simmer, partly covered, for 15 minutes.

...

Add fish, and shrimp (if using), and poach for a few minutes (times depend on types of fish and shellfish used, so stagger the time when you add them to the pot) until flesh is opaque and cooked through.

...

Serve soup steaming hot, with one of the following garnishes if desired.

SERVING SUGGESTIONS

Place a slice of toasted bread rubbed with garlic in bottom of soup bowl and ladle serving of soup over top. Drizzle with olive oil.

...

Garnish with gremolata (a mixture of grated lemon rind, chopped fresh parsley and minced garlic).

4

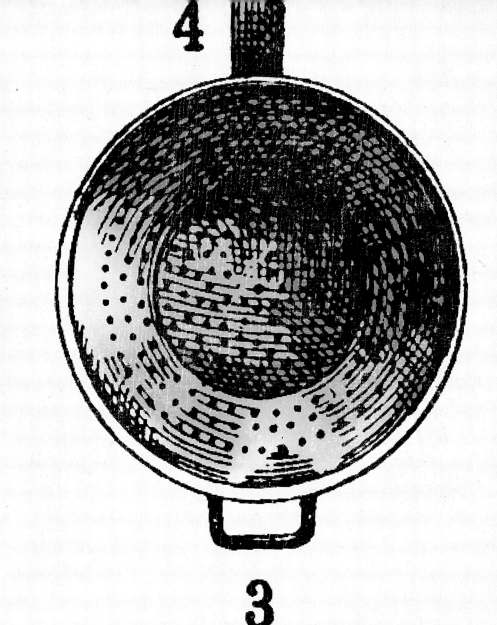

3

LA PASTA

AND NOW FOR SOME PASTA!

This chapter contains 50 pasta recipes and almost as many variations. There are recipes here for all seasons and tastes. No matter the occasion, whether you want an express dish or one that simmers for hours, you'll find one that suits you.

In the pages that follow, a few basic rules will help you make very good pasta. Once you learn them, it really is simple.

PASTA TYPES AND PORTIONS

Choose hard semolina pasta (*semola di grano duro*). In Italy, pasta is often served as an appetizer, in portions of about 3 oz (90 g). All the recipes in this book use dry pasta (*pasta secca*) because you can get it anywhere and it's easy to keep in your pantry. You may certainly use fresh pasta if you feel like it. You can even try your hand at making it, using the recipe on p. 174.

COOKING

Pasta is cooked, uncovered, in a large amount of water so it can move freely. For 4 portions, use a large pot (6- to 7-quart /6 to 7 L capacity), preferably made of stainless steel. Salt water generously after bringing it to a boil. Salt added to cold water drops to the bottom of the pot, potentially damaging the metal. The amount you add is a matter of taste, but please note that if there is not enough salt in the water, it is very difficult to adjust the seasoning later.

...

Never put oil in the cooking water (except when boiling lasagna noodles) because it prevents the sauce from sticking to the pasta. Stir at the beginning of cooking and occasionally thereafter to prevent clumping. When should you start cooking the pasta? Only when the sauce is finished or nearly finished, unless it's extra-quick to prepare. Pasta can't wait – you have to wait for the pasta!

COOKING TIME

Taste a noodle shortly before the time suggested on the package. The best way to enjoy pasta is al dente, or still slightly firm to the bite.

RESERVING COOKING WATER

Before draining, reserve 1/2 cup (125 mL) of the water used to cook the pasta. You can use some to thin the sauce or make it smoother if necessary – plus, it helps the sauce evenly coat the pasta. But be sure not to drown the noodles! If pasta is to be cooked further in sauce or soup, drain before the time recommended on the package. Leave a little water on the noodles to prevent sticking and help blend the sauce. Never rinse cooked pasta unless you'll be eating it cold in a salad.

SAUCE

Generally speaking, you should pour the sauce into a large warmed serving bowl, then add the pasta and mix well so that the noodles get coated with sauce and start soaking it up. Do not drown noodles in sauce; they should be merely "coloured."

BEFORE SERVING

Use the pepper mill at the last minute for sharper flavour. You can also stir in a few spoonfuls of butter to make the sauce silkier. Put a bottle of your very best cold-pressed extra-virgin olive oil on the table and let your guests help themselves. And at the last minute, garnish pasta with a handful of fresh herbs or serve with a small salad for added flavour, colour and texture.

...

Put grated cheese such as Parmesan, grana Padano or Pecorino Romano (see Glossary, p. 182) on the table for everyone to use as desired. In Italy, cheese is not traditionally served with seafood, fish or mushroom sauces, but I believe that this, too, is a matter of taste.

MOST IMPORTANTLY, IMPROVISE

I offer a few noodle suggestions for each sauce, but let yourself be charmed by the names and myriad shapes available.

+ stelline (little stars) +
+ farfalle (bow ties) +
+ capelli d'angelo (angel hair) +
+ cappelletti (little hats) +
+ anellini (little rings) +
+ fiori (flowers) +
+ penne (quills) +
+ lumache (snails) +

BASIC TOMATO SAUCE

This is your base, which you can modify to suit the day, the season or whatever happens to be on hand. It's a good sauce to keep in the freezer. In the off-season, rather than using flavourless supermarket tomatoes, you're better off opening a can of plum tomatoes.

SERVES 4

3 tbsp (45 mL) olive oil
+ 1 or 2 cloves garlic, chopped
+ 1 can (28 oz/796 mL) diced tomatoes, or whole tomatoes, chopped
+ Sugar, to taste (optional)
+ 1/4 cup (50 mL) chopped Italian flat-leaf parsley
+ Salt and freshly ground pepper
+ 1/2 cup (125 mL) chopped fresh basil

In a saucepan, heat oil over low heat and infuse garlic for 3 to 4 minutes without browning.

...

Add tomatoes, sugar (if using), and parsley. Season with salt and pepper to taste.

...

Simmer over medium-low heat, partly covered, for 20 minutes or until desired consistency. The cover may be removed toward the end of cooking to thicken the sauce. Add basil. Adjust seasoning.

...

You can freeze this tomato sauce in airtight containers for up to 6 months. When reheating, make sure you cook for enough time that the frozen condensation evaporates and the sauce is not watery.

SERVING SUGGESTIONS

Replace basil with a melange of snipped fresh herbs. Or add 1 tsp (5 mL) dried Italian herb seasoning or herbes de Provence at the beginning of cooking.

...

For a spicy sauce, add hot pepper sauce or hot pepper flakes to taste.

VARIATION

Fresh Tomato Sauce: Prepare Basic Tomato Sauce, replacing canned tomatoes with 12 plump, ripe plum tomatoes. Peel, seed and chop tomatoes (see p. 179) before adding to pot. Increase cooking time slightly to obtain desired consistency.

TOMATO AND MOZZARELLA SAUCE

Everyone, young and old, adores stretchy mozzarella cheese. Try this recipe – you'll love it.

SERVES 4

6 to 8 oz (175 to 250 g) mozzarella di bufala or mozzarina cheese
+ Olive oil or herbed olive oil
+ 1 batch Basic Tomato Sauce (see p. 56)
+ 1/2 cup (125 mL) grated Parmesan or Pecorino Romano cheese
+ Freshly ground pepper
+ Fresh basil

Dice mozzarella and drizzle with oil.
...
Heat tomato sauce over medium heat. Add Parmesan and mozzarella cheeses. Heat until cheese melts.
...
Mix immediately with cooked pasta.

TO SERVE

If desired, season with pepper and garnish with basil. Serve *subito* (right now!), as this dish will not wait.

TOMATO AND GINGER SAUCE

That's right, ginger! Its compatibility with tomatoes was a great discovery.

1 batch Basic Tomato Sauce (see p. 56)
+ 2 tbsp (30 mL) grated gingerroot
+ A few spoonfuls of butter

Replace basil in basic recipe with ginger and blend in butter.

SERVING SUGGESTION

Have fun with the ingredients to create new variations. Use your imagination – open the pantry or go to the market or your own garden to concoct a tomato sauce with onion, fennel or leeks. Or vary the herbs by adding thyme, rosemary, etc.

RAW TOMATO SAUCE

I suggest you celebrate the all-too-short tomato season to excess with this recipe.
Today, you'll find more varieties than ever at the market. You can't go wrong with plump,
fragrant tomatoes. The hot pasta will highlight their full flavour.

SERVES 4

2 lb (1 kg) field tomatoes or 12 to
16 plum tomatoes*

+ 1 tsp (5 mL) salt

+ 1/2 cup (125 mL) olive oil

+ 1/2 cup (125 mL) snipped fresh herbs
   (such as basil, mint, chives or Italian
   flat-leaf parsley), or to taste

+ Salt and freshly ground pepper

+ Grated Parmesan cheese

*You can also make this sauce with quartered
cherry or grape tomatoes, or a variety of
tomatoes in different colours.

Skin tomatoes (see p. 179) if desired.
It is not necessary to remove the
skin of in-season or fully ripe
tomatoes. With or without skin,
seed tomatoes and dice. Place in
sieve, add salt and let drain for
10 minutes.

…

Combine tomatoes and oil in a large
bowl. Let rest for at least 30 minutes
at room temperature.

…

Add herbs or one of the garnishes
suggested on right. Mix well. Season
with salt and pepper to taste.

…

Before serving, mix with cooked
spaghettini or short pasta and
sprinkle with Parmesan cheese.

SERVING SUGGESTIONS

With olives and capers: Add 3/4 cup
(175 mL) thinly sliced pitted green
or black olives; 2 tbsp (30 mL)
capers, drained, rinsed, patted dry
and chopped; and 1 to 2 tsp (5 to
10 mL) grated lemon or orange rind.
Top with shaved Parmesan rather
than grated.

…

With arugula: Add a few handfuls of
arugula along with the herbs.

…

With cheese: Dice 8 oz (250 g) fresh
mozzarella or bocconcini and
season with salt, pepper and a
drizzle of olive oil. Add to pasta once
it is cooled by the tomatoes.

…

With garlic: Gently heat 1/2 cup
(125 mL) olive oil and infuse 3 or
4 cloves garlic, quartered, for 6 to
7 minutes without browning.
Remove garlic, let oil cool and
pour over tomatoes. In spring, use
new garlic, simply chopped raw.

TOMATO SAUCE
WITH CARAMELIZED ONIONS

Imagine all the velvety sweetness of caramelized onions in a tomato sauce.
Trust me, this is a recipe you'll make often.

SERVES 4 TO 6

2 tbsp (30 mL) butter

+ 2 tbsp (30 mL) olive oil

+ 2 Spanish or red onions, sliced

+ 1 clove garlic, crushed or minced

+ 1 can (28 oz/796 mL) diced tomatoes,
   or whole tomatoes, chopped

+ 2 tsp (10 mL) fresh rosemary or 1/2 tsp
   (2 mL) dried

+ 1/4 tsp (1 mL) hot pepper flakes,
   or to taste

+ Salt and freshly ground pepper

+ Grated or shaved Pecorino Romano or
   Parmesan cheese

In a skillet, heat butter and oil. Fry onions over medium heat, stirring often, for about 20 minutes or until golden and caramelized. Remove one-quarter of the caramelized onions and set aside for garnish.

...

Add garlic, tomatoes, rosemary and hot pepper flakes. Season with salt and pepper to taste. Simmer, uncovered, for 20 minutes.

TO SERVE

Serve pasta coated with onion sauce. Top with reserved onions and cheese.

SERVING SUGGESTION

With eggplant: Mix sauce with penne or other short pasta and serve on a bed of roasted eggplant (see p. 172).

PASTA WITH HERBS AND CHERRY TOMATOES

A natural-gas stove provides a precise flame and instant heat, which maintain and even enhance the flavour of the tomatoes in this quick pasta dish. This cooking method is both simple and refined, just like Italian cuisine.

SERVES 4

2 packages (each 10 oz/285 g) cherry or grape tomatoes
+ 1/4 cup (50 mL) olive oil
+ 2 cloves garlic, halved
+ 1/4 to 1/2 tsp (1 to 2 mL) hot pepper flakes (optional)
+ Salt
+ 1 cup (250 mL) chopped Italian flat-leaf parsley
+ 1/2 cup (125 mL) chopped fresh mint or basil
+ 1 lb (500 g) spaghettini or other pasta
+ Freshly ground pepper
+ Grated or shaved Parmesan or Pecorino Romano cheese

Cut tomatoes in half and press slightly to extract juice. Set aside.

…

In a large skillet, warm oil over low heat and infuse garlic for 4 to 5 minutes without browning.

…

Add tomatoes, and hot pepper flakes (if using). Season with salt to taste. Cook over medium-low heat for 4 to 5 minutes. Remove garlic and add parsley and mint.

…

Meanwhile, in a large pot of boiling salted water, cook pasta according to package instructions. Drain, reserving 1/2 cup (125 mL) of the cooking water.

…

In same pot, mix pasta and tomato mixture, adding a little of the reserved cooking water if necessary to coat pasta well. Season with salt and pepper to taste.

…

Before serving, sprinkle with Parmesan cheese.

SERVING SUGGESTIONS

With arugula: Replace mint with 2 cups (500 mL) chopped arugula.

…

With olives: Add 16 quartered pitted green or black olives to finished sauce.

…

With shallots: Replace garlic with 1/2 cup (125 mL) chopped French shallots.

PENNE ALL'ARRABBIATA

This pasta can be more or less "angry" (the meaning of *arrabbiata*) depending on the chef's tastes.
In season, use small fresh hot peppers instead of the dried, but take care –
each pepper has its own distinct aroma and heat. Ricotta helps tame the fieriness.
Bonus: This sauce can be made in less than 10 minutes.

SERVES 4 OR 5

1/3 cup (75 mL) olive oil

+ 4 anchovy fillets, rinsed, patted dry
  and chopped

+ 1/2 tsp (2 mL) hot pepper flakes

+ 2 to 4 cloves garlic, minced

+ 2 cans (each 14 oz/398 mL) diced
  tomatoes, or whole tomatoes, chopped

+ 1/2 cup (125 mL) chopped Italian
  flat-leaf parsley

+ 1 tbsp (15 mL) tomato paste

+ Salt

+ 1 lb (500 g) penne or other short pasta

+ Grated Parmesan cheese

In a skillet, warm oil over medium-low heat. Add anchovies, hot pepper flakes and garlic and infuse for about 30 seconds without browning garlic.

…

Add tomatoes, parsley and tomato paste and stir well.

…

Season lightly with salt, as anchovies are salty. Simmer over low heat for 5 minutes.

…

Meanwhile, in a large pot of boiling salted water, cook pasta according to package instructions. Drain.

…

In a warmed serving bowl, mix sauce and a little Parmesan cheese. Add hot pasta and stir to coat.

TO SERVE

Sprinkle with more Parmesan cheese.

SERVING SUGGESTIONS

With shrimp: Sauté shrimp in a little oil. Season with salt and pepper to taste and serve over pasta.

…

With ricotta: Add a heaping spoonful of ricotta and a drizzle of olive oil and mix well.

ELENA'S PRESERVED TOMATOES

When plum tomatoes are at their best and fill Jean Talon market in Montreal, you're sure to meet
Elena Faita there. She will show you how to prolong summer by making preserves.
The secret lies in choosing good, plump, ripe plum tomatoes.
Be sure to follow proper sterilizing techniques. Tomatoes also freeze very well;
just cook them a little longer to evaporate any frozen condensation, which can make them watery.

WHEN, WHICH ONES AND HOW MANY?

In cooler temperate climates, like Quebec, tomato season starts in mid-August. Italian Romanello, San Marzano or Roma tomatoes give the best results. A 22-lb (10 kg) basket yields twenty 2-cup (500 mL) jars. Before processing tomatoes, lay them out on a bedsheet and let them ripen for 2 to 4 days. You'll also need two nice, fat bunches of fresh basil.

...

Peel and seed tomatoes (see p. 179). Cut each in half.

...

Sterilize jars thoroughly and fill with tomato halves. Add 2 or 3 basil leaves to each jar. Press tomatoes down gently with a fork before adding more to pack them down and prevent air bubbles from forming. Leave about 1 inch (2.5 cm) headspace between the tomatoes and the lid.

...

Before putting on the lid, wipe rims of jars. Screw on lids. It is very important not to overtighten them.

...

Place in a large pot, separating jars with a dishcloth to prevent breakage. Cover with water.

...

To sterilize, bring to a boil and simmer for 15 to 20 minutes.

...

Remove from heat and let jars cool in pot until water is lukewarm.

...

Remove jars, wipe dry and tighten lids to ensure a good seal.

...

The juices from the tomatoes accumulate at the bottom of the jars first, but after 2 or 3 days, the tomatoes will sink and the juices will rise to the top. This juice is also delicious in recipes, so don't waste it.

...

Store jars in a cool place (not the refrigerator).

IMPORTANT NOTE

Once the jars of tomatoes have been boiled and sterilized, the lids must be perfectly sealed to be safe. To ensure tomatoes are vacuum-sealed, press lid down slightly – it shouldn't move. Store any jars that aren't vacuum-sealed in the refrigerator and use up quickly.

PESTO

Pesto artfully captures the freshness and flavour of good ingredients. The word *pesto* comes from the Italian *pestare,* meaning "to mash or to crush." Basil pesto, traditionally made in a mortar, is said to be one of the oldest Italian sauces. Since you probably already have your own favourite recipe, I propose other types of pesto here, and there is one for every taste. USE Pesto enhances pasta, fish, grilled meat or soup. It is also a terrific accompaniment to raw vegetables, a fantastic crostini topping and more. Add pesto just before serving to preserve the full flavour. STORAGE In an airtight container, covered with a thin layer of oil, pesto will keep for a few days in the fridge. Sun-dried tomato pesto will stay fresh a bit longer. All the pestos, except those made with rapini or arugula, can be frozen in small containers or ice cube trays to make individual servings. Once frozen, the pesto cubes can be transferred to freezer bags. Thaw them in the refrigerator as needed. Having pesto on hand is an excellent idea; remembering to use it is an even better one!

———————

WALNUT PESTO

This is a good pesto, which you'll use in the recipe for Walnut Pasta and Pan-Fried Mushrooms (see p. 80) and in Roasted Squash Pasta (see p. 118).

MAKES 1 1/4 CUPS (300 ML)

1 cup (250 mL) walnut halves, toasted for 5 minutes and cooled

+ 1 cup (250 mL) Italian flat-leaf parsley

+ 1/2 cup (125 mL) grated Parmesan cheese

+ A pinch of chopped garlic or 3 or 4 cloves Roasted Garlic (see p. 170)

+ A pinch of hot pepper flakes

+ Salt and freshly ground pepper

+ About 1/2 cup (125 mL) olive oil

In a food processor, coarsely chop walnuts and parsley. Add Parmesan, garlic, hot pepper flakes, and salt and pepper to taste. Gradually add oil to food processor, pulsing several times, until pesto is blended but not too smooth. Texture should remain coarse.

SERVING SUGGESTIONS

Add to a chicken salad or to a beet-and-endive salad.

...

Blend with fresh goat cheese and spread on bread.

SUN-DRIED TOMATO PESTO

Sun-dried tomatoes are easier to eat when chopped, as they are here. This pesto suits any season and any occasion. Try it on its own or blended into a spread for canapés, on hot or cold pasta, or as a flavour booster in tomato sauce, soups, sandwiches and even stews. It also makes a delicious and welcome gift. After several tries, I've come up with this very simple recipe, which preserves the full flavour of the tomatoes. You can also experiment with the variations.

MAKES 3/4 CUP (175 ML)
1 cup (250 mL) oil-packed sun-dried tomatoes (see p. 179)
+ 1/2 cup (125 mL) fresh basil leaves
+ About 1/3 cup (75 mL) olive oil, or oil from the tomatoes
+ Salt and freshly ground pepper

Drain tomatoes. If they're packed in good-quality oil, you can save it to prepare the pesto.
…

Chop tomatoes and basil in a food processor. Add the extra ingredients if you are making one of the variations (right). Gradually add oil to food processor, pulsing several times, until pesto is blended but not too smooth, so that the chunks of tomato can still be tasted. Season with salt and pepper to taste.

NOTE
You can finely chop the tomatoes with a knife or mezzaluna instead of a food processor if you prefer.

VARIATIONS
Cheese, Nut and Sun-Dried Tomato Pesto: Add 1/4 cup (50 mL) grated Parmesan or Pecorino Romano cheese and 1/4 cup (50 mL) lightly toasted pine nuts or slivered almonds (see p. 173).
…

Garlic Sun-Dried Tomato Pesto: Add a hint of chopped fresh garlic, or 3 or 4 cloves Roasted Garlic (see p. 170).
…

Hot Sun-Dried Tomato Pesto: Add a pinch of hot pepper paste or flakes, or other hot spices or hot sauce.
…

Olive and Sun-Dried Tomato Pesto: Add 1/3 cup (75 mL) pitted black olives.

PISTACHIO-ARUGULA PESTO

This very rich, flavour-packed pesto will appeal to everyone who loves arugula.
I count myself among them!

MAKES 1 1/2 CUPS (375 ML)

4 cups (1 L) arugula, stems removed

+ 1 cup (250 mL) pistachios, roasted for 4 to 5 minutes (see p. 173)

+ 1/2 cup (125 mL) grated Parmesan cheese or equal parts Parmesan and Romano cheeses

+ Chopped garlic, to taste

+ Salt and freshly ground pepper

+ About 1/2 cup (125 mL) olive oil

In a food processor, coarsely chop arugula, pistachios, Parmesan and garlic. Season with salt and pepper to taste. Gradually add oil to food processor, pulsing several times, until pesto is blended but not too smooth. Texture should remain coarse.

TO SERVE

Spread on crostini and top with mozzarella or bocconcini cheese.

...

Enjoy simply with tomatoes.

...

Add to pasta, thinning pesto with a little of the pasta cooking liquid or some mascarpone cheese.

VARIATION

Pine Nut–Arugula Pesto: Replace pistachios with pine nuts.

SAGE PESTO

This unusual pesto is perfect for stuffed pasta, poultry and soups. You'll find plenty of other uses for it, too.

MAKES 1 1/4 CUPS (300 ML)

1 clove garlic, chopped, or 3 cloves Roasted Garlic (see p. 170)

+ 1 cup (250 mL) toasted walnuts (see p. 173)

+ 1/2 cup (125 mL) chopped Italian flat-leaf parsley

+ 5 to 6 tbsp (75 to 90 mL) chopped fresh sage

+ Salt

+ About 1/2 cup (125 mL) olive oil

+ 1/2 cup (125 mL) grated Parmesan cheese

In a food processor, coarsely chop garlic, walnuts, parsley and sage. Season with salt to taste. Gradually add oil to food processor, pulsing several times, until pesto is blended but not too smooth. Texture should remain coarse.

...

Add cheese and pulse enough to blend in.

TO SERVE

Toss with ravioli or tortellini.

...

Use to garnish a vegetable soup or squash bisque.

...

Enjoy simply on vegetables.

RAPINI PESTO

This recipe comes from Marie-Fleur Saint-Pierre, chef at the Montreal restaurant Tapéo, who uses it as a topping for fish. I've adapted the recipe for pasta. The bitterness of the rapini is toned down by the nuts. You can serve it as is or thin it with a few spoonfuls of mascarpone cheese.

MAKES 2 CUPS (500 ML)

1 bunch rapini, florets and stems separated
+ 1 or 2 cloves garlic, chopped, or 4 or 5 cloves Roasted Garlic (see p. 170)
+ 1/2 cup (125 mL) lightly toasted pecans (see p. 173)
+ Hot pepper flakes, to taste (optional)
+ Salt and freshly ground pepper
+ About 1/2 cup (125 mL) olive oil

In a large pot of boiling salted water, immerse rapini stems for about 45 seconds, then add florets for another 20 seconds. Drain well, pressing out excess liquid, and chop coarsely.

...

In a food processor, coarsely chop rapini, garlic, pecans, and hot pepper flakes (if using). Season with salt and pepper to taste. Gradually add oil to food processor, pulsing several times, until pesto is blended but not too smooth. Texture should remain coarse.

TO SERVE

Combine with ravioli, tortellini or short pasta. Garnish with Parmesan cheese shavings and, if desired, toasted pecans.

VARIATION

Rapini Pesto with Lemon or Anchovy: Add grated lemon zest or mashed anchovy fillets to taste.

WALNUT PASTA AND PAN-FRIED MUSHROOMS

This is for anyone who prefers a sauce without cream. With walnut pesto on hand, all you need to do is fry the mushrooms. And any variety of mushrooms will do the trick.

SERVES 4 OR 5

3 tbsp (45 mL) olive oil

+ 1 lb (500 g) mushrooms (such as portobello, cremini, oyster or shiitake), thinly sliced
+ Salt
+ A pinch of hot pepper flakes, or to taste (optional)
+ 1 lb (500 g) long or short pasta of your choice
+ Walnut Pesto* (see p. 74)
+ Freshly ground pepper

*Calculate one generous spoonful of pesto per serving.

In a large skillet, heat 2 tbsp (30 mL) of the oil over medium-high heat and add half of the mushrooms. Season with salt to taste, and a few of the hot pepper flakes (if using). Allow mushrooms to brown for several minutes, adding a little more of the remaining olive oil as necessary. When the mushrooms are nicely coloured on both sides, remove from the skillet. Repeat with remaining mushrooms. Keep warm.

…

In a large pot of boiling salted water, cook pasta according to package instructions. Drain, reserving 1/2 cup (125 mL) of the cooking water.

…

Toss pasta, pesto and some of the reserved cooking water until pasta is well coated.

…

Serve pasta on individual plates, topped with pan-fried mushrooms. Season with pepper to taste.

SERVING SUGGESTIONS

Replace mushrooms with fried butternut squash or zucchini.

…

Serve alongside a salad of pear tomatoes seasoned with grated lemon zest and olive oil.

ZUCCHINI-FETA GEMELLI

In Italy, zucchini is often prepared with ricotta salata cheese. This cheese can be difficult to find in Canada, so I suggest replacing it with feta. The mint pesto in this recipe binds the ingredients together nicely.

SERVES 4

2 tbsp (30 mL) olive oil

+ 2 or 3 cloves garlic, cut in half

+ 5 small zucchini*

+ Salt

+ 1 lb (500 g) gemelli or other pasta

+ 6 oz (175 g) feta or ricotta salata cheese, crumbled

+ Mint Pesto (see below)

+ A handful of toasted pine nuts (see p. 173)

+ Freshly ground pepper

*Choose fairly slender zucchini so that they do not make the sauce watery.

In a large skillet, heat oil over low heat and infuse garlic for 4 to 5 minutes without browning. Remove garlic from oil.

…

Cut zucchini lengthwise into quarters, then into 1/2-inch (1 cm) thick slices.

…

Add zucchini to skillet and season with salt to taste. Sauté over medium heat for 5 minutes or until light golden but still crisp. Add a little more oil if necessary.

…

In a large pot of boiling salted water, cook pasta according to package instructions. Drain, reserving 1/2 cup (125 mL) of the cooking water.

…

Toss pasta, feta and pesto in a large serving bowl. Add zucchini and stir well, adding a little of the reserved cooking water if necessary to moisten. Adjust seasoning.

TO SERVE

Garnish with pine nuts and season with pepper to taste.

MINT PESTO

MAKES 2/3 CUP (150 ML)

3/4 cup (175 mL) packed mint leaves

+ 2 tbsp (30 mL) feta or ricotta salata cheese

+ 1/2 tsp (2 mL) hot pepper flakes (optional)

+ Grated rind and juice of 1 lemon

+ Salt and freshly ground pepper

+ About 1/3 cup (75 mL) olive oil

In a food processor, coarsely chop mint, feta, hot pepper flakes (if using), and lemon rind and juice. Season with salt and pepper to taste. Gradually add oil to food processor, pulsing several times, until pesto is blended but not too smooth. Texture should remain coarse.

NOTE

Ricotta salata is firm and saltier than fresh ricotta. It's worth trying if you can find it.

TUNA AND SUN-DRIED TOMATO SPAGHETTI

In my family, we regularly have this recipe on weeknights. The taste of the flavourful oil-packed tuna, the zingy lemon and the refreshing arugula or basil make it a favourite all around.

SERVES 2

1/4 cup (50 mL) homemade (see p. 76) or store-bought sun-dried tomato pesto*

+ Finely grated rind of 1 lemon
+ Juice of 1/2 lemon
+ A splash of olive oil
+ 15 to 20 black olives, pitted and chopped
+ 7 oz (200 g) long or short pasta of your choice
+ Salt and freshly ground pepper
+ 1 can (7 oz/198 g) oil-packed tuna, drained and flaked
+ A generous handful of snipped Italian flat-leaf parsley, arugula or basil, to taste

*If you do not have pesto, use finely chopped oil-packed sun-dried tomatoes.

In a bowl, combine pesto, lemon rind and juice, oil and olives.

...

In a large pot of boiling salted water, cook pasta according to package instructions. Drain, reserving 1/4 cup (50 mL) of the cooking water.

...

Toss hot pasta and pesto mixture. Add a little of the reserved cooking water, if necessary, to coat pasta well with sauce. Season with salt and pepper to taste.

...

Add tuna and gently combine.

TO SERVE

Garnish with parsley.

STUFFED PASTA

Pasta can be shaped in countless ways (think of agnolotti, tortellini, cappelletti, ravioli...) and stuffed as the chef fancies. If possible, pasta filled with cheese, vegetables or meat should be purchased fresh. Frozen stuffed pasta makes a very good alternative, though, and keeping some on hand allows you to whip up a meal in almost no time, since a quick sauce makes it into a meal. Do not cook stuffed pasta in rapidly boiling water or it will fall apart. Remove from the pot with a slotted spoon or a small sieve and set on a heated plate before gently coating in sauce.

————————

BAY AND CREAM RAVIOLI

Hurray for bay! Here, the classic seasoning takes on a starring role.

SERVES 4

1 can (14 oz/398 mL) beef consommé
+ 1 cup (250 mL) 35% whipping cream or 15% country-style cream*
+ 6 to 8 bay leaves
+ 1 lb (500 g) fresh or frozen ravioli
+ Grated Parmesan cheese
+ Salt and freshly ground pepper

*Country-style cream is thicker than regular 15% cream and is often used for cooking.

In a large saucepan, bring consommé, cream and bay leaves to a boil. Let infuse over low heat, uncovered, for 30 minutes.

...

In a large pot of boiling salted water, cook ravioli until al dente. Remove with a slotted spoon and transfer to sauce to finish cooking. Adjust seasoning.

TO SERVE

Sprinkle with Parmesan and pepper to taste.

SERVING SUGGESTIONS

Stuffed pasta can be served in all sorts of ways, including:
– with a pesto made from basil or walnuts (see p. 74), arugula and pistachios (see p. 77) or rapini (see p. 78);
– with Aglio e Olio sauce (see p. 123);
– with any of the many tomato sauces in this book.

SUN-DRIED TOMATO BUTTER RAVIOLI

This dish is a guaranteed palate-pleaser. It's appetizing, ready in a flash and bursting with flavour.

SERVES 4

1/4 cup (50 mL) butter

+ Finely grated rind of 1 lemon
+ 1/4 cup (50 mL) homemade (see p. 76) or store-bought sun-dried tomato pesto
+ 1 lb (500 g) fresh or frozen ravioli
+ Grated Parmesan or Pecorino Romano cheese
+ Salt and freshly ground pepper

<u>In a large skillet</u>, melt butter over low heat. Add lemon rind and pesto and mix well.

…

<u>In a large pot of boiling salted water</u>, cook ravioli according to package instructions. Remove with a slotted spoon and transfer to butter mixture. Stir to combine. Adjust seasoning.

TO SERVE

Sprinkle with Parmesan and pepper to taste.

SAGE BUTTER RAVIOLI

The great classics stand the test of time without losing any of their appeal. This dish is surprisingly simple in its ingredients and cooking method, and the sauce is one of my favourites for ravioli.

SERVES 4

1/4 cup (50 mL) butter or equal parts butter and olive oil

+ 24 fresh sage leaves
+ 1 lb (500 g) fresh or frozen ravioli
+ Grated or shaved Parmesan cheese
+ Salt and freshly ground pepper

<u>In a skillet</u> over very low heat, melt butter. Add sage leaves and let infuse for 5 minutes to flavour butter.

…

<u>In a large pot of boiling salted water</u>, cook ravioli according to package instructions. Remove with a slotted spoon and transfer to butter mixture. Reserve 1/2 cup (125 mL) of the cooking water.

…

<u>Gently combine</u> ravioli mixture, adding a little of the reserved cooking water if necessary to coat ravioli well. Adjust seasoning and serve immediately.

TO SERVE

Sprinkle with Parmesan and pepper to taste.

ASPARAGUS AND GREEN PEA RAVIOLI

We celebrate the arrival of the first spring vegetables at our markets with a touch of ginger or hot pepper.

SERVES 4

1/4 cup (50 mL) butter

+ 2 tbsp (30 mL) olive oil
+ 1 cup (250 mL) chopped slender asparagus (1-inch/2.5 cm pieces)
+ 1 cup (250 mL) thawed or fresh green peas
+ 1 tbsp (15 mL) grated gingerroot, or hot pepper flakes to taste
+ Salt and freshly ground pepper
+ 1 lb (500 g) fresh or frozen ravioli
+ Grated or shaved Parmesan cheese

<u>In a skillet</u>, heat butter and oil over medium heat. Sauté asparagus and peas. Add ginger. Pour in a few spoonfuls of water and continue cooking until vegetables are tender-crisp. Season with salt and pepper to taste.

…

<u>In a large pot of boiling salted water</u>, cook ravioli according to package instructions. Remove with a slotted spoon and transfer to butter mixture. Reserve 1/2 cup (125 mL) of the cooking water.

…

<u>Gently combine</u> ravioli mixture, adding a little of the reserved cooking water if necessary to coat ravioli well. Adjust seasoning and serve immediately.

TO SERVE

Sprinkle with Parmesan and pepper to taste.

SPEEDY CLAM SPAGHETTINI

In Italy, this delicious dish is made with tiny fresh clams. Here is a pantry version made with small canned clams that tastes wonderful nonetheless.

SERVES 4

2 tbsp (30 mL) olive oil

+ 2 or 3 large shallots or 6 green onions, finely chopped
+ 2 or 3 cloves garlic, finely chopped
+ Hot pepper flakes or hot pepper paste, to taste
+ 1 cup (250 mL) clam juice or fish stock
+ Salt
+ 1 lb (500 g) spaghettini or other long pasta
+ 2 cans (each 5 oz/142 mL) small clams, drained
+ 2 to 3 tbsp (30 to 45 mL) butter
+ Snipped Italian flat-leaf parsley, to taste
+ Finely grated lemon rind, to taste (optional)
+ Freshly ground pepper

Heat oil in a skillet over medium heat and cook shallots for 2 minutes.

...

Add garlic and hot pepper flakes. Pour in clam juice. Bring to a boil and simmer over medium-high heat for 2 minutes to reduce. Season with salt to taste.

...

Meanwhile, in a large pot of boiling salted water, cook pasta according to package instructions. Drain.

...

Stir clams into sauce and pour over pasta. Add butter and parsley. Toss until pasta is well coated.

TO SERVE

Sprinkle with lemon rind (if using) and pepper.

SHRIMP SPAGHETTINI

This light, colourful and flavourful pasta dish features perfectly tender shrimp.

SERVES 4

2 plum tomatoes, seeded and diced, or
1 cup (250 mL) cherry tomatoes,
quartered and seeded
+ 2 cups (500 mL) watercress or arugula,
   or 1 cup (250 mL) Italian flat-leaf
   parsley, coarsely chopped
+ Juice (optional)* and grated rind of
   1 lemon
+ Salt
+ 1/4 cup (50 mL) olive oil
+ 1 lb (500 g) peeled deveined medium
   shrimp, cut in halves or thirds
+ 2 or 3 cloves garlic, finely chopped
+ 1/4 tsp (1 mL) hot pepper flakes, or to
   taste
+ 1/2 cup (125 mL) white wine or white
   vermouth such as Noilly Prat
+ 1 lb (500 g) spaghettini or other long
   pasta
+ 2 to 4 tbsp (30 to 60 mL) butter
+ Freshly ground pepper

*Add the lemon juice if you like a tangier
flavour.

In a small bowl, combine tomatoes, watercress and lemon rind. Season with salt to taste. Set aside.

...

Heat 2 tbsp (30 mL) of the oil in a large skillet over high heat. Pat shrimp dry and season with salt to taste. Sear until shrimp turn pinkish. Transfer shrimp to plate and keep warm.

...

Reduce heat and add remaining oil to skillet. Cook garlic and hot pepper flakes for 2 minutes. Deglaze skillet with white wine and lemon juice (if using). Remove from heat.

...

Meanwhile, in a large pot of boiling salted water, cook pasta according to package instructions.

...

Drain, reserving 1/2 cup (125 mL) of the cooking water.

...

Return pasta to pot and add shrimp, wine mixture and tomato mixture. Toss, adding a little of the reserved cooking water if necessary, until pasta is well coated. Stir in butter and season with salt and pepper to taste.

VARIATION

Sausage and Shrimp Spaghettini: Add sliced cured sausage, such as cacciatora or chorizo, along with sautéed shrimp.

TOMATO AND MEATBALL SAUCE

My grandmother had a trick that I'll share with you: save some meatballs and enjoy them later in a sandwich.

SERVES 6 TO 8

MEATBALLS

1/2 cup (125 mL) crumbs from stale bread (no crusts) chopped in food processor, or 1/4 cup (50 mL) dry bread crumbs
+ About 1/4 cup (50 mL) milk or water
+ 1 lb (500 g) mixture of ground veal and pork
+ 2 large eggs, lightly beaten
+ 1 clove garlic, pressed
+ 2/3 cup (150 mL) grated Parmesan cheese or a blend of grated Pecorino Romano and Parmesan cheeses
+ 1/4 cup (50 mL) snipped Italian flat-leaf parsley
+ 1/4 tsp (1 mL) ground nutmeg
+ Your choice of seasoning:
  – 1/3 cup (75 mL) snipped fresh basil
  – 1 tsp (5 mL) dried Italian herb seasoning or herbes de Provence
  – 1 tbsp (15 mL) finely grated lemon rind
+ Salt and freshly ground pepper
+ A little olive oil for frying

SAUCE

1/4 cup (50 mL) olive oil
+ 2 cloves garlic, chopped
+ 1 can (28 oz/796 mL) diced tomatoes, or whole tomatoes, chopped
+ 1 can (14 oz/398 mL) diced tomatoes, or whole tomatoes, chopped
+ 1/2 cup (125 mL) snipped Italian flat-leaf parsley
+ 1/2 cup (125 mL) chicken stock
+ A little sugar (optional)*
+ A pinch of hot pepper flakes (optional)
+ 1 tbsp (15 mL) chopped fresh basil, or 1 tsp (5 mL) dried Italian herb seasoning or herbes de Provence
+ Grated Parmesan cheese
+ Freshly ground pepper

*Add if tomatoes taste too acidic.

MEATBALLS

In a large bowl, combine bread crumbs with enough milk to moisten well. Let stand for 5 minutes. Add ground veal and pork, eggs, garlic, Parmesan cheese, parsley and nutmeg, along with your choice of seasoning. Season with salt and pepper to taste. Combine until well mixed. Fry a small amount of the mixture; taste and adjust seasoning if necessary.
...

Shape mixture into 1 1/2-inch (4 cm) meatballs. In a large deep skillet, heat a little oil over medium-high heat and brown meatballs. Do not cook too many at a time. Drain fat from skillet if necessary between batches. When finished, return all meatballs to skillet.

SAUCE

In a large bowl, combine oil, garlic, tomatoes, parsley, stock, sugar (if using), and hot pepper flakes (if using). Pour over meatballs and simmer over low heat, half-covered, for about 1 hour. Check to make sure sauce is not too thick, adding water if necessary. Add basil at the last minute.

TO SERVE

Place your choice of cooked pasta in a warmed serving bowl. Toss with just enough sauce to barely coat pasta. Serve pasta with a little more sauce spooned over top and garnished with meatballs. Sprinkle with Parmesan cheese and pepper.

NOTE

You can freeze the sauce and the meatballs together for up to 2 months.

SERVING SUGGESTION

Serve meatballs with cooked broccoli, rapini or Chinese broccoli instead of pasta. Drizzle a thin stream of olive oil over vegetables and sprinkle with grated Parmesan cheese.

PASTA BOLOGNESE

A traditional bolognese sauce simmers gently for three hours. I've created this faster-cooking version to save time. Adding butter and cheese to the sauce just before serving makes it exceptionally rich-tasting.

SERVES 4 OR 5

1 tbsp (15 mL) olive oil

+ About 1/4 cup (50 mL) butter

+ 1 onion, chopped

+ 1 or 2 carrots, diced

+ 1 or 2 stalks celery or 1/2 bulb fennel, diced

+ 1 lb (500 g) mixed ground meat* (such as pork, veal or a mix of the two)

+ 2 oz (60 g) pancetta or prosciutto, finely chopped (optional)

+ Salt

+ 1 cup (250 mL) milk

+ 1 cup (250 mL) white wine

+ 1/2 to 3/4 tsp (2 to 4 mL) ground nutmeg

+ 1 cup (250 mL) canned diced tomatoes, or canned whole tomatoes, chopped

+ Chopped fresh basil or Italian flat-leaf parsley, to taste (optional)

+ 1 lb (500 g) rigatoni or other pasta

+ Grated Parmesan cheese

+ Freshly ground pepper

*Meat should be coarsely ground. Ask the butcher to put it through the meat grinder only once.

Heat oil and 2 tbsp (30 mL) of the butter in a skillet over medium heat. Sauté onion, carrots and celery for 4 to 5 minutes.

...

Add ground meat, and pancetta (if using), and cook over high heat until meat is no longer pink. Season with salt to taste.

...

Pour in milk and simmer for 5 to 8 minutes or until almost completely evaporated.

...

Add wine and nutmeg. Simmer, letting sauce reduce, for about 10 minutes.

...

Add tomatoes. Reduce heat to low and cook for 60 to 90 minutes, stirring occasionally. Adjust seasoning and thin sauce with a little water if too thick. At the end of cooking, add basil (if using).

...

Meanwhile, in a large pot of boiling salted water, cook pasta according to package instructions. Drain.

...

Transfer sauce to a large warmed serving bowl. Add remaining butter, adding a little extra if necessary, and a lot of Parmesan cheese. Stir until well combined.

...

Add pasta to bowl and toss to coat well with sauce. Season with salt and pepper to taste and serve immediately.

VARIATION

Porcini Pasta Bolognese: Add finely chopped thawed or rehydrated porcini mushrooms along with the tomatoes.

PASTA ALLA GENOVESE

My TV crew and I will always associate this dish with a wonderful day spent at Paola and Giampaolo Motta's vineyard, La Massa, located in Italy's magnificent Chianti region. There we were in the heart of Tuscany, cooking a Neapolitan recipe named for the city of Genoa. Three geographical regions in one dish! In Italy, this type of recipe is eaten in two courses: the first is pasta with only the juices from the meat, and the second is the meat with a vegetable or salad.

SERVES 6 TO 8

2 tbsp (30 mL) olive oil
+ 2 tbsp (30 mL) butter
+ 2 lb (1 kg) bone-in beef roast (such as shoulder, blade or cross-rib)
+ Salt and freshly ground pepper
+ 4 lb (2 kg) onions, halved and thinly sliced (about 16 medium onions)
+ 5 oz (150 g) sliced prosciutto, diced*
+ 1 lb (500 g) bucatini or other long pasta
+ Grated Pecorino Romano or Parmesan cheese

*Ask for slices about 1/8 inch (3 mm) thick.

In a large heavy-bottomed pot, heat oil and butter over medium-high heat. Sear beef on all sides. Season with salt and pepper to taste.

...

Add onions and prosciutto, spreading them evenly around the pot.

...

Cover and cook over very low heat for 6 to 8 hours, basting meat several times. Alternatively, bake meat in the centre of a 250°F (120°C) oven.

...

Remove lid for the last half hour of cooking or remove meat from pot after cooking and reduce cooking juices in saucepan over medium-high heat until about 3 cups (750 mL) remain.

...

In a large pot of boiling salted water, cook pasta according to package instructions.

...

Meanwhile, remove bone from beef and shred meat by pulling with two forks. Keep warm.

...

Drain pasta. Return to pot and stir in a little of the beef cooking juices. Season with salt and pepper to taste and reheat pasta for about 1 minute.

TO SERVE

Serve the pulled beef on the pasta. Sprinkle with Pecorino Romano cheese and pepper.

SUNDAY RAGÙ

Ragù is a slowly and gently cooked meat sauce. Almost every Italian has memories of eating this dish on Sunday at Grandma's, and every family has its own recipe. Traditionally, like Pasta alla Genovese (see p. 100), this dish is served in two courses: the sauce and pasta as *primo piatto*, and the meat with a salad or braised green vegetable as *secondo*. Here, everything is eaten in one single course.

SERVES 6

3 cups (750 mL) beef or chicken stock
+ 3/4 oz (25 g) dried porcini mushrooms*
+ 1/4 cup (50 mL) olive oil
+ 1 large onion, diced
+ 1 stalk celery, diced
+ 1 carrot, diced (optional)
+ 2 to 4 cloves garlic, smashed
+ 1 lb (500 g) pork spareribs
+ 2 or 3 mild or hot Italian sausages
+ About 1 lb (500 g) bone-in veal, beef or lamb roast (such as shoulder or blade)
+ Salt and freshly ground pepper
+ 1 cup (250 mL) red wine
+ 1 can (28 oz/798 mL) whole tomatoes, diced or chopped
+ 1 bay leaf
+ 1 lb (500 g) pasta of your choice
+ Chopped Italian flat-leaf parsley, to taste

*For a rosemary version, replace porcini mushrooms with 3 sprigs rosemary and add them along with the bay leaf.

Preheat oven to 350°F (180°C).

...

In a small saucepan, bring 1 cup (250 mL) of the stock to a boil. Remove from heat and add porcini mushrooms; soak for at least 20 minutes. Place a sieve lined with paper towel over a bowl. Strain mushrooms, reserving soaking liquid. Chop mushrooms and set aside.

...

In a large heavy-bottomed ovenproof pot, heat 2 tbsp (30 mL) of the oil over medium heat and gently sauté onion, celery and carrot for about 5 minutes. Add reserved mushrooms and garlic and continue cooking for 2 minutes. Remove vegetables from pot and set aside.

...

Cut spareribs into 2-rib pieces.

...

In the same pot, heat remaining oil over medium-high heat and sear spareribs, sausages and veal on all sides. Season with salt and pepper to taste. Add wine and cook over medium heat until slightly reduced. Add tomatoes, remaining stock, mushroom soaking liquid and bay leaf. Add reserved vegetables. Season with salt to taste.

...

Cover and bake in the oven for 2 1/2 to 3 hours or until veal falls off the bone. During cooking, add water as necessary to keep from drying out.

...

In a large pot of boiling salted water, cook pasta according to package instructions. Drain, reserving 1/2 cup (125 mL) of the cooking water.

...

Remove bone from veal. Place veal, spareribs and sausages in a warmed serving dish and combine with a little of the cooking juices.

...

In another large warmed serving dish, toss pasta with a small amount of the meat cooking juices, adding reserved cooking water as necessary, until well coated. Season with salt and pepper to taste.

TO SERVE

Sprinkle pasta with parsley. Place pasta and meat dishes on table and serve from both.

SUNDAY RAGÙ

Ragù is a slowly and gently cooked meat sauce. Almost every Italian has memories of eating this dish on Sunday at Grandma's, and every family has its own recipe. Traditionally, like Pasta alla Genovese (see p. 100), this dish is served in two courses: the sauce and pasta as *primo piatto,* and the meat with a salad or braised green vegetable as *secondo.* Here, everything is eaten in one single course.

SERVES 6

3 cups (750 mL) beef or chicken stock
+ 3/4 oz (25 g) dried porcini mushrooms*
+ 1/4 cup (50 mL) olive oil
+ 1 large onion, diced
+ 1 stalk celery, diced
+ 1 carrot, diced (optional)
+ 2 to 4 cloves garlic, smashed
+ 1 lb (500 g) pork spareribs
+ 2 or 3 mild or hot Italian sausages
+ About 1 lb (500 g) bone-in veal, beef or lamb roast (such as shoulder or blade)
+ Salt and freshly ground pepper
+ 1 cup (250 mL) red wine
+ 1 can (28 oz/798 mL) whole tomatoes, diced or chopped
+ 1 bay leaf
+ 1 lb (500 g) pasta of your choice
+ Chopped Italian flat-leaf parsley, to taste

*For a rosemary version, replace porcini mushrooms with 3 sprigs rosemary and add them along with the bay leaf.

Preheat oven to 350°F (180°C).

…

In a small saucepan, bring 1 cup (250 mL) of the stock to a boil. Remove from heat and add porcini mushrooms; soak for at least 20 minutes. Place a sieve lined with paper towel over a bowl. Strain mushrooms, reserving soaking liquid. Chop mushrooms and set aside.

…

In a large heavy-bottomed ovenproof pot, heat 2 tbsp (30 mL) of the oil over medium heat and gently sauté onion, celery and carrot for about 5 minutes. Add reserved mushrooms and garlic and continue cooking for 2 minutes. Remove vegetables from pot and set aside.

…

Cut spareribs into 2-rib pieces.

…

In the same pot, heat remaining oil over medium-high heat and sear spareribs, sausages and veal on all sides. Season with salt and pepper to taste. Add wine and cook over medium heat until slightly reduced. Add tomatoes, remaining stock, mushroom soaking liquid and bay leaf. Add reserved vegetables. Season with salt to taste.

…

Cover and bake in the oven for 2 1/2 to 3 hours or until veal falls off the bone. During cooking, add water as necessary to keep from drying out.

…

In a large pot of boiling salted water, cook pasta according to package instructions. Drain, reserving 1/2 cup (125 mL) of the cooking water.

…

Remove bone from veal. Place veal, spareribs and sausages in a warmed serving dish and combine with a little of the cooking juices.

…

In another large warmed serving dish, toss pasta with a small amount of the meat cooking juices, adding reserved cooking water as necessary, until well coated. Season with salt and pepper to taste.

TO SERVE

Sprinkle pasta with parsley. Place pasta and meat dishes on table and serve from both.

SAUSAGE AND SUN-DRIED TOMATO PASTA

This fast, very tasty dish requires little effort but has lots of personality.

SERVES 4

1 lb (500 g) hot or mild Italian sausages
+ 2 tbsp (30 mL) olive oil
+ 1 cup (250 mL) wine or chicken stock
+ 2 tbsp (30 mL) tomato paste
+ Salt and freshly ground pepper
+ 1 lb (500 g) orecchiette or other short pasta
+ 1/4 cup (50 mL) chopped oil-packed sun-dried tomatoes or sun-dried tomato pesto
+ 4 cups (1 L) arugula, baby arugula or baby spinach, chopped (optional)

Remove casings from sausages. In a large skillet, heat oil over medium heat and cook sausage meat, breaking up chunks with a fork, for 5 minutes or until no longer pink. Drain fat from pan.

...

Stir in wine and tomato paste. Season with salt and pepper to taste. Simmer over low heat for 10 minutes.

...

Meanwhile, in a large pot of boiling salted water, cook pasta according to package instructions. Drain, reserving 1/2 cup (125 mL) of the cooking water.

...

Return pasta to pot and add sun-dried tomatoes and sauce. Toss, adding reserved cooking water as necessary, until pasta is well coated.

...

Add arugula (if using). Season with salt and pepper to taste and serve immediately.

SAUSAGE AND FENNEL PASTA

My mother made this recipe regularly, but never exactly the same way! Sometimes she added a little pesto, sometimes leeks. Here is one of the many variations.

SERVES 4 OR 5

1 lb (500 g) hot or mild Italian sausages, or a mix of the two
+ 1/4 cup (50 mL) olive oil
+ 1 bulb fennel (see p. 173), halved and thinly sliced
+ 2 sweet red peppers, thinly sliced
+ 1 clove garlic, chopped
+ 1/2 to 1 tsp (2 to 5 mL) fennel seeds, crushed
+ 1/4 tsp (1 mL) hot pepper flakes
+ Salt and freshly ground pepper
+ 1 lb (500 g) short pasta of your choice
+ About 1/2 cup (125 mL) chicken stock
+ Grated or shaved Parmesan or Pecorino Romano cheese

Remove casings from sausages. In a large skillet, heat 2 tbsp (30 mL) of the oil over medium heat and cook sausage meat, breaking up chunks with a fork, for 5 minutes or until no longer pink. Transfer meat to plate and keep warm. Drain fat from pan.

...

Add remaining oil to skillet and sauté sliced fennel and peppers for 3 to 4 minutes. Add garlic, fennel seeds and hot pepper flakes and continue cooking for 2 minutes. Season with salt and pepper to taste.

...

In a large pot of boiling salted water, cook pasta according to package instructions. Drain and return to pot.

...

Meanwhile, pour stock into skillet. Add reserved meat and bring to a boil.

...

Toss pasta and sauce together in the pot. Season with salt and pepper to taste.

TO SERVE

Sprinkle with Parmesan cheese.

GREEN PEA AND PROSCIUTTO PASTA

This colourful, simple dish is surprisingly flavourful. Try it!

SERVES 4

3 tbsp (45 mL) olive oil

+ 2 tbsp (30 mL) butter

+ 1 large onion, chopped

+ 5 oz (150 g) sliced prosciutto*, julienned

+ 2 cups (500 mL) thawed or fresh green peas, blanched for 30 seconds in boiling salted water

+ Hot pepper flakes, to taste (optional)

+ 1 lb (500 g) farfalle or other short pasta

+ A large handful of fresh mint or Italian flat-leaf parsley, snipped

+ Grated Parmesan cheese

+ Freshly ground pepper

*Ask butcher to slice prosciutto about 1/8 inch (3 mm) thick.

In a large skillet, heat oil and butter over medium heat and sauté onion until translucent, being careful not to let it brown.

...

Add prosciutto and green peas and cook for 2 to 3 minutes. Season with hot pepper flakes (if using).

...

In a large pot of boiling salted water, cook pasta according to package instructions. Drain, reserving 1/2 cup (125 mL) of the cooking water. Return pasta to pot.

...

Add pea mixture to pasta along with mint. Toss, adding reserved cooking water as necessary, until pasta is well coated.

TO SERVE

Garnish with more mint. Sprinkle with Parmesan cheese and pepper.

SPAGHETTI ALLA CARBONARA

Traditionally, this dish is made with guanciale (see Glossary, p. 184),
but I replace it here with pancetta or bacon. *Alla carbonara* means "coal-miner-style."
Is it because you grind lots of fresh black pepper onto the dish before eating it or
because a coal miner invented it? Who knows – it's delicious either way.

SERVES 2

8 oz (250 g) spaghetti, fettuccine or
linguine
+ A little olive oil
+ 1/4 cup (50 mL) diced pancetta or
  bacon
+ 2 large eggs
+ About 1/4 cup (50 mL) grated
  Parmesan cheese
+ Freshly ground pepper

In a large pot of boiling salted
water, cook pasta according to
package instructions. Drain,
reserving 1/2 cup (125 mL) of the
cooking water.

...

Meanwhile, in a large skillet, heat
oil over medium-high heat and
sauté pancetta until crisp. Add a
little of the reserved cooking water
to the skillet to tenderize meat.

...

In a large serving bowl, mix eggs
and Parmesan cheese with a fork.
Season with pepper to taste.

...

Stir pasta into pancetta. Pasta
should be very hot. Transfer to
serving bowl and toss to coat well
with sauce.

TO SERVE

Sprinkle with more Parmesan
cheese.

CARBONARA WITH VEGETABLES

After enjoying this dish made by my friend Jean Fortin, I adopted it. This recipe allows you to vary the vegetables according to the season.

SERVES 4 OR 5

2 heads garlic

+ 4 large eggs

+ 2 tbsp (30 mL) olive oil

+ 2 onions, halved and thinly sliced

+ 1 large bulb fennel (see p. 173), halved and thinly sliced

+ 3 zucchini, julienned or halved lengthwise and thinly sliced

+ Salt

+ 1 lb (500 g) pasta of your choice

+ About 3/4 cup (175 mL) grated Parmesan cheese

+ Freshly ground pepper

+ A handful of fresh basil, baby spinach or arugula, shredded

Begin by roasting garlic (see p. 170). Squeeze roasted garlic cloves from skins and mash into a purée.

...

In a bowl, whisk eggs with 1/4 cup (50 mL) of the roasted garlic purée.

...

In a large skillet, heat oil over medium-high heat and cook onions and fennel until lightly caramelized. Add zucchini and season with salt to taste. Continue cooking for 2 minutes.

...

In a large pot of boiling salted water, cook pasta according to package instructions. Drain, reserving 1/2 cup (125 mL) of the cooking water.

...

In a large warmed serving bowl, toss pasta with vegetables. Add Parmesan cheese and egg mixture. Season with pepper to taste. Toss, adding reserved cooking water as necessary, until pasta is well coated. Add basil.

TO SERVE

Sprinkle with more Parmesan cheese and season with pepper to taste.

SERVING SUGGESTIONS

With asparagus: In the spring, replace zucchini with chopped asparagus.

...

With zucchini blossoms: In the summer, garnish dish with sautéed zucchini blossoms.

MUSHROOM PAPPARDELLE

My friend Marie-Claude Goodwin often serves this sauce. I've shared the recipe
with many friends, and now we all make it.

SERVES 4

1 1/4 cups (300 mL) chicken stock
+ 1/2 oz (15 g) dried porcini mushrooms
+ About 2 to 3 tbsp (30 to 45 mL) olive oil
+ 1 onion, chopped
+ 2 cloves garlic, chopped
+ 6 to 8 slices prosciutto, chopped
+ 14 oz (425 g) fresh mushrooms (such
  as portobello, shiitake, oyster or
  cremini), sliced
+ Salt and freshly ground pepper
+ 1/4 cup (50 mL) 35% whipping cream
+ 1 lb (500 g) pappardelle or other pasta
+ Snipped Italian flat-leaf parsley,
  to taste
+ Grated Parmesan cheese

In a small saucepan, bring stock to a boil. Remove from heat and add porcini mushrooms; soak for at least 20 minutes. Place a sieve lined with paper towel over a bowl. Strain mushrooms, reserving soaking liquid. Chop mushrooms and set aside.

…

In a large skillet, heat oil over medium-high heat and cook onion until golden. Add garlic and continue cooking for 1 minute. Add prosciutto and cook for 2 minutes. Transfer mixture to plate and keep warm.

…

In the same skillet, heat a little more oil over high heat and sauté fresh mushrooms until golden. If necessary, cook in 2 batches, adding a little more oil between batches. Season with salt and pepper to taste, then add reserved porcini mushrooms. Return onion mixture to pan and continue cooking over medium heat for 4 to 5 minutes to develop flavours.

…

Add reserved soaking liquid and cream. Simmer over medium heat for a few seconds, then reduce heat to low. Keep warm.

…

In a large pot of boiling salted water, cook pasta according to package instructions. Drain.

…

In a large warmed serving bowl, toss pasta with mushroom sauce and parsley until well coated. Season with salt and pepper to taste and serve immediately.

…

TO SERVE

Sprinkle with Parmesan cheese.

CAULIFLOWER PENNE

Natalia Ravida taught me to make this dish when I visited her family olive grove in Sicily for my TV show. I'd tried several times without much success to create a similar recipe, so her expertise was welcome. Thank you, Natalia! She shares other recipes in her cookbook, *Seasons of Sicily* (New Holland Publishers, 2007).

SERVES 4

1 cauliflower, cut into small florets*
+ 3 tbsp (45 mL) olive oil
+ 1 onion, halved and thinly sliced
+ Hot pepper flakes, to taste
+ 1/4 cup (50 mL) raisins
+ 3 tbsp (45 mL) pine nuts, or to taste
+ 3 or 4 anchovy fillets, rinsed, patted
  dry and chopped
+ 2 pinches of saffron
+ Salt
+ A drizzle of olive oil
+ Freshly ground pepper
+ 1 lb (500 g) penne or other short pasta
+ 1 cup (250 mL) grated caciocavallo,
  Pecorino Romano or Parmesan cheese

*Add some colour by using yellow or green cauliflower.

In the pot that will be used to cook the pasta, bring a large amount of water to a boil and add salt. Cook cauliflower for 5 minutes or until tender-crisp. Using a slotted spoon or sieve, transfer cauliflower to a bowl and set aside. Reserve cooking water in pot to cook pasta.

...

In another large pot, heat oil over medium heat and add onion and hot pepper flakes. Cook for 5 minutes or until onion is translucent.

...

Add raisins and pine nuts and continue cooking for 2 minutes. Add anchovies, mashing into mixture with a fork. Add reserved cauliflower, saffron and 1/2 cup (125 mL) of the reserved cooking water. Season with salt to taste.

...

Cook for 10 minutes or until cauliflower is tender enough to mash with a fork. Adding a thin stream of oil and a little more of the cooking water as necessary, mash cauliflower until smooth. Season with salt and pepper to taste.

...

Meanwhile, bring reserved cooking water to a boil. Cook pasta according to package instructions. Drain, reserving 1/2 cup (125 mL) of the cooking water.

...

Add cauliflower sauce to pasta. Season with salt and pepper to taste. Toss pasta, drizzling with a thin stream of olive oil and reserved cooking water as necessary, until pasta is well coated with sauce. Sprinkle with cheese; toss and serve immediately.

BROCCOLI-TURMERIC FETTUCCINE

This recipe combines broccoli and turmeric, two popular cancer-fighting foods, with a hint of curry for an Indian-inspired culinary journey. Since curry powders and pastes vary in strength, you decide on the amount to use.

SERVES 4

1 head broccoli

+ 3 tbsp (45 mL) olive oil
+ 2 cloves garlic, halved
+ 2 shallots, chopped
+ 1 tsp (5 mL) turmeric
+ 1 to 1 1/2 tsp (5 to 7 mL) curry paste
  or powder
+ Salt
+ 1/2 cup (125 mL) 35% whipping cream
+ 1 lb (500 g) fettuccine or other pasta
+ Grated Parmesan cheese
+ Freshly ground pepper
+ A large handful of toasted pine nuts
  (see p. 173)

Cut broccoli into 1 1/2-inch (4 cm) florets. Peel stalk and cut into 1/2-inch (1 cm) cubes.

...

In the pot that will be used to cook the pasta, bring a large amount of water to a boil and add salt. Cook broccoli for 1 minute or until bright green. Using a slotted spoon or sieve, transfer broccoli to a bowl and set aside. Reserve cooking water in pot to cook pasta.

...

In a skillet, heat oil over low heat and cook garlic and shallots gently for 4 to 5 minutes without browning. Remove garlic.

...

Add turmeric, curry paste and reserved broccoli to skillet. Season with salt to taste. Add cream and 1/4 cup (50 mL) of the reserved cooking water. Simmer for 2 minutes or until broccoli is tender-crisp.

...

Meanwhile, bring reserved cooking water to a boil. Cook pasta according to package instructions. Drain, reserving 1/2 cup (125 mL) of the cooking water.

...

Add broccoli mixture to pasta and toss, adding reserved cooking water as necessary, until pasta is well coated with sauce.

...

Sprinkle with Parmesan cheese and toss. Season with salt and pepper to taste.

...

TO SERVE

Garnish with pine nuts.

ROASTED SQUASH PASTA

This colourful dish already has many fans. I suggest two pestos here,
but almost any kind of pesto will do the trick.

SERVES 4

4 slices pancetta or bacon (optional)

+ 1 butternut squash (2 lb/1 kg)

+ 1 onion, quartered

+ Olive oil

+ Salt and freshly ground pepper

+ 8 oz (250 g) cherry or pear tomatoes

+ Hot pepper flakes (optional)

+ 1 lb (500 g) short pasta of your choice

+ Sage Pesto (see p. 77) or Walnut Pesto (see p. 74)*

+ Shaved Parmesan or grana Padano cheese

*Calculate one generous spoonful of pesto per serving.

Preheat oven to 400°F (200°C).

...

If using pancetta, arrange slices on a parchment paper–lined baking sheet. Bake in the oven for 10 minutes or until crisp. Let drain on paper towel–lined plate. Set aside.

...

Meanwhile, cut squash in half and scoop out seeds with a spoon. Cut squash into large chunks; peel with a vegetable peeler or paring knife. Cut into small cubes to make about 5 cups (1.25 L).

...

On a baking sheet, toss together squash, onion quarters and a little of the olive oil. Season with salt and pepper to taste. Bake in the oven for 30 to 40 minutes, turning halfway through cooking.

...

Halve tomatoes and gently squeeze between fingers to drain off a little of the juice. Drizzle lightly with oil. About 10 minutes before squash is done, add tomatoes, and hot pepper flakes (if using), to baking sheet. Remove from oven and set aside.

...

In a large pot of boiling salted water, cook pasta according to package instructions. Drain, reserving 1/2 cup (125 mL) of the cooking water.

...

In the same pot or a warmed serving dish, toss the pasta, pesto and a little of the reserved cooking water until pasta is well coated. Add reserved roasted vegetables.

...

TO SERVE

Garnish with Parmesan shavings and crumbled pancetta (if using).

ROASTED GARLIC AND RED PEPPER FETTUCCINE

This savoury recipe comes from my friend Stéphan Boucher. Each person decides how much roasted garlic to mash into the cooked peppers.

SERVES 4 OR 5

1/2 cup (125 mL) olive oil
+ 12 cloves garlic, peeled and halved
+ 1 red onion, chopped
+ 3 sweet red peppers, with or without peel (see p. 176), diced or cut in strips
+ 1/4 cup (50 mL) chopped oil-packed sun-dried tomatoes
+ 1 cup (250 mL) red wine or beef stock
+ Hot pepper flakes, to taste
+ Salt
+ 1 lb (500 g) fettuccine or other long pasta
+ 1/3 cup (75 mL) chopped fresh chives or Italian flat-leaf parsley
+ Freshly ground pepper
+ Grated or shaved ricotta salata or Parmesan cheese

In a large skillet, heat oil over medium-low heat and sauté garlic, stirring often, for 5 minutes or until soft. Do not let garlic brown. Using slotted spoon, remove from pan and set aside.

...

Add onion, red peppers and sun-dried tomatoes to pan and cook for 10 minutes. Add wine and hot pepper flakes. Season with salt to taste.

...

Meanwhile, in a large pot of boiling salted water, cook pasta according to package instructions. Drain.

...

Add red pepper mixture, chives and pepper to pasta and toss gently. Serve immediately.

TO SERVE

Garnish with reserved roasted garlic and ricotta salata cheese.

AGLIO E OLIO

In Italy, this dish is nicknamed "midnight pasta" because it's so easy to prepare from just a few pantry staples. While the pasta cooks, you prepare the flavoured oil. Go easy on the garlic and hot pepper or heap it on – it's your choice! As a rule, Italians don't add cheese, but there's nothing stopping you.

SERVES 4

1 lb (500 g) spaghettini or other long thin pasta

+ 1/3 to 1/2 cup (75 to 125 mL) olive oil
+ 2 to 4 cloves garlic, finely chopped
+ 1/2 cup (125 mL) chopped Italian flat-leaf parsley
+ 1/4 tsp (1 mL) hot pepper flakes, or to taste
+ Salt and freshly ground pepper

In a large pot of boiling salted water, cook pasta according to package instructions.

...

Meanwhile, in a large skillet, heat oil over low heat and infuse garlic for 3 to 4 minutes without browning. Add parsley and hot pepper flakes. Set aside.

...

Drain pasta, reserving 1/2 cup (125 mL) of the cooking water.

...

Add pasta to reserved flavoured oil. Toss, adding reserved cooking water as necessary, until pasta is well coated. Season with salt and pepper to taste. Serve immediately.

VARIATIONS

Aglio e Olio with Spinach: Before draining pasta, add 1 bag (10 oz/ 300 g) fresh baby spinach or regular spinach, chopped, to pot. Drain with pasta and combine with flavoured oil.

...

Aglio e Olio with Anchovies: Mash anchovy fillets and add along with hot pepper flakes.

CACIO E PEPE

This recipe appeared in my first book, but I'm including it here again since it is a classic bit of Italian cooking.

SERVES 4

1 lb (500 g) long pasta of your choice

+ 2 to 4 tbsp (30 to 60 mL) butter or olive oil, or equal parts of each
+ 2 tsp (10 mL) black peppercorns, crushed
+ 1 1/3 cups (325 mL) grated Pecorino Romano or Parmesan cheese, or equal parts of each
+ Finely grated lemon rind and lemon juice, to taste (optional)

In a large pot of boiling salted water, cook pasta according to package instructions.

...

Meanwhile, place butter and pepper in a hot serving dish. To keep it hot, you can set the dish on the pot of cooking pasta.

...

Drain pasta, reserving 1 cup (250 mL) of the cooking water.

...

Transfer pasta to the hot serving dish and toss with peppery butter until well coated.

...

Gradually stir in 1 cup (250 mL) of the cheese, adding reserved cooking water as necessary to moisten.

TO SERVE

Garnish with remaining cheese, and lemon rind and juice (if using).

LEMON PASTA

For empty-fridge days, here is another pasta recipe that's elegant and simple.
A splash of oil, a handful of Parmesan and some lemon – that's it. You can serve
this pasta as an appetizer or a side dish, too. Since lemon oils are volatile,
grate the lemon rind at the last minute to preserve its flavour.

**SERVES 8 AS AN APPETIZER
OR 4 AS A MAIN COURSE**

Finely grated rind of 3 room-temperature lemons (organic if possible)
+ Juice of 2 lemons
+ 1 1/3 cups (325 mL) grated Parmesan cheese
+ 5 tbsp (75 mL) olive oil
+ 1 lb (500 g) spaghettini or other long thin pasta
+ Salt and freshly ground pepper
+ A good handful of fresh basil, snipped

*You may need other ingredients if making one of the variations on the far right.

In a large bowl, combine lemon rind and juice, Parmesan and oil. Set aside.

...

In a large pot of boiling salted water, cook pasta according to package instructions. Drain, reserving 1/2 cup (125 mL) of the cooking water.

...

Add hot pasta to lemon sauce. Season with salt and pepper to taste. Toss, adding reserved cooking water as necessary, until pasta is well coated with sauce.

TO SERVE

Garnish with basil.

VARIATIONS

Lemon and Onion Pasta: In skillet, heat equal parts olive oil and butter over medium heat. Sauté 2 onions, chopped, until translucent. Do not let brown. Add to pasta along with other ingredients.

...

Lemon Asparagus Pasta: In the water to be used for cooking pasta, cook 1 lb (500 g) asparagus, trimmed, until tender. Remove with a slotted spoon and rinse under cold running water; chop. To reheat, add to pasta for the last few minutes of cooking.

...

Lemon Seafood Pasta: In Italy, seafood is never served with Parmesan. This lemon pasta is delicious nonetheless when topped with shrimp or scallops sautéed in olive oil with salt, pepper and hot pepper flakes to taste.

RICOTTA AND HERB PASTA

This summer dish, which bursts with freshness, comes from a friend by the name of Louisa Pesant. Try your own combination of herbs – it will be just as good.

SERVES 4

3/4 cup (175 mL) ricotta or cottage cheese

+ 1/2 cup (125 mL) grated Parmesan cheese
+ 5 tbsp (75 mL) butter, softened
+ 1/4 cup (50 mL) chopped fresh basil
+ 3 tbsp (45 mL) chopped Italian flat-leaf parsley
+ 2 tbsp (30 mL) chopped fresh chives
+ 1/2 tsp (2 mL) finely grated lemon rind
+ 1 tbsp (15 mL) lemon juice
+ 1 lb (500 g) gemelli or other short pasta
+ Salt and freshly ground pepper
+ Fresh herb leaves (such as basil, parsley and/or chives)

In a food processor*, pulse ricotta, Parmesan cheese, butter, basil, parsley, chives, and lemon rind and juice until smooth. Set aside.

…

In a large pot of boiling salted water, cook pasta according to package instructions. Drain, reserving 1/2 cup (125 mL) of the cooking water.

…

Return pasta to pot along with herb-cheese mixture. Season with salt and pepper to taste. Toss, adding reserved cooking water as necessary, until pasta is well coated with sauce. Adjust seasoning.

*You can finely chop the herbs by hand with a chef's knife instead, then combine them with the other sauce ingredients. If using cottage cheese, however, you'll need the food processor to ensure a smooth texture.

TO SERVE

Garnish with fresh herb leaves.

HAM, MASCARPONE AND ARUGULA PASTA

Another recipe for a quick and frankly delicious meal. The name says it all!

SERVES 4 OR 5

1 lb (500 g) short pasta of your choice
+ 2 to 3 tbsp (30 to 45 mL) butter
+ 7 oz (200 g) speck-style smoked ham
  (see p. 184) or prosciutto, diced
+ 6 cups (1.5 L) arugula, coarsely
  chopped
+ 1 cup (250 mL) mascarpone cheese or
  crème fraîche
+ Salt and freshly ground pepper
+ Grated Parmesan cheese

In a large pot of boiling salted water, cook pasta according to package instructions.

…

Meanwhile, in a large skillet, melt butter over medium heat. Add ham and arugula; cook until hot and arugula is slightly wilted. Remove from heat and stir in mascarpone. Season with salt and pepper to taste. Mix well.

…

Drain pasta, reserving 1/2 cup (125 mL) of the cooking water. Add pasta to sauce. Toss, adding reserved cooking water as necessary, until pasta is well coated.

TO SERVE

Sprinkle with Parmesan cheese and pepper.

NOTE

If you have any leftover mascarpone, try a very appetizing chocolate dip (see p. 146) at another meal.

VARIATION

Replace arugula with baby spinach, or cooked fresh or thawed frozen green peas.

PASTA AU GRATIN

This is mac and cheese in its Sunday best! The good news is that you don't need to make a white sauce. The recipe calls for aged Cheddar cheese, but feel free to blend in other cheeses.

SERVES 6

3 cups (750 mL) shredded extra-old Cheddar cheese

+ 2 cups (500 mL) 35% whipping cream or 15% country-style cream*

+ 1 can (14 oz/398 mL) diced tomatoes, or whole tomatoes, chopped

+ 1 1/2 cups (375 mL) grated Parmesan or Pecorino Romano cheese

+ 1 large bunch fresh basil, chopped

+ Salt and freshly ground pepper

+ 1 lb (500 g) tortiglioni or other short pasta

+ 1/2 cup (125 mL) dry bread crumbs

+ A splash of olive oil

*Country-style cream is thicker than regular 15% cream and is often used for cooking.

Preheat oven to 400°F (200°C). In a large bowl, mix Cheddar cheese, cream, tomatoes, 1 cup (250 mL) of the Parmesan cheese and basil. Season with salt and pepper to taste. Set aside.

...

In a large pot of boiling salted water, cook pasta until almost al dente. Drain well.

...

Add pasta to cheese mixture and stir to combine.

...

Divide pasta mixture evenly among six 1 1/2-cup (375 mL) ramekins or spread in a large casserole dish.

...

Mix bread crumbs, remaining Parmesan cheese and olive oil. Sprinkle over top. Bake in the oven for 12 to 15 minutes for ramekins or 25 to 30 minutes for casserole dish.

SERVING SUGGESTION
Serve with a salad of fresh greens.

MACARONI BAMBINI

I wanted an ultra-simple, orange-coloured pasta dish for kids. Here's what my friend Stéphan Boucher suggested. If they don't like Parmesan, leave it out – but not all of it!

SERVES 6 TO 8 CHILDREN

1 lb (500 g) ruote (wagon wheels) or other short pasta
+ 2 large eggs
+ 3 cups (750 mL) shredded mild Cheddar cheese
+ 1/2 cup (125 mL) grated Parmesan cheese
+ 2 tbsp (30 mL) tomato paste
+ Salt and freshly ground pepper
+ Roasted tomatoes (see p. 179), optional

In a large pot of boiling salted water, cook pasta according to package instructions.

...

Meanwhile, beat eggs in a bowl. Add Cheddar cheese, Parmesan cheese and tomato paste. Season with salt and pepper to taste. Mix well.

...

Drain pasta, reserving 1/2 cup (125 mL) of the cooking water.

...

Return pasta to pot and add cheese mixture. Toss, adding reserved cooking water as necessary, until pasta is well coated.

...

Reheat until pasta is hot and cheese is melted. Adjust seasoning.

TO SERVE

Garnish with roasted tomatoes (if using). You can also place the macaroni under the broiler for a gratin-style finish.

SERVING SUGGESTIONS

For grown-ups: Season generously with pepper and add spinach wilted in olive oil.

...

For little ones: Add small cooked broccoli florets.

SPINACH AND BLUE PENNE

This easy blue-cheese sauce is rich and creamy, and the spinach lends a note of freshness. I use this recipe to showcase the talents of many artisanal cheese producers. If you can use your own locally produced cheese, so much the better!

SERVES 4 OR 5

1 lb (500 g) penne or other short pasta

+ 1 cup (250 mL) 35% whipping cream or chicken stock

+ 7 oz (200 g) Gorgonzola or your favourite local artisanal blue cheese, crumbled

+ 2 cups (500 mL) baby spinach or baby arugula

+ 1/3 cup (75 mL) chopped toasted nuts (see p. 173), such as walnuts, pecans or pistachios

+ Freshly ground pepper

In a large pot of boiling salted water, cook pasta according to package instructions. Drain, reserving 1/2 cup (125 mL) of the cooking water.

...

Meanwhile, in a small saucepan, heat cream. Add cheese, mashing with a fork but leaving small lumps.

...

Return pasta to pot and pour sauce over top. Toss, adding reserved cooking water as necessary, until pasta is well coated with sauce. Quickly mix in spinach and nuts. Serve immediately.

TO SERVE

Season generously with pepper.

EGGPLANT-RICOTTA LASAGNA

Of course, lasagna takes some time to make, but if you prepare it in advance,
you can feed a gang simply by turning on the oven and tossing a salad.

SERVES 8

A double batch of Basic Tomato Sauce
(see p. 56)

+ Hot pepper flakes, to taste

+ 3 lb (1.5 kg) eggplants

+ 1 tbsp (15 mL) olive oil

+ Salt

+ 1 lb (500 g) ricotta cheese

+ 1 1/2 cups (375 mL) grated Parmesan
  cheese

+ 2 large eggs, lightly beaten

+ 1/2 tsp (2 mL) grated nutmeg

+ Freshly ground pepper

+ 1 lb (500 g) fresh lasagna noodles or
  12 oz (375 g) dried lasagna noodles

+ 2 cups (500 mL) shredded provolone or
  mozzarella cheese

+ 2 cups (500 mL) shredded mozzarella
  cheese

Prepare tomato sauce ahead of time,
adding hot pepper flakes. Set aside.

...

Peel eggplants and cut into 1/4-inch
(5 mm) thick rounds (if eggplants
are small, cut into strips). Brush
with oil, sprinkle with salt and broil
on baking sheet for 4 minutes per
side or until golden. Set aside.

...

Preheat oven to 350°F (180°C).

...

In a bowl, mix ricotta cheese, 1 cup
(250 mL) of the Parmesan cheese,
eggs and nutmeg. Season with salt
and pepper to taste.

...

In a large pot of boiling salted water
with a bit of oil added, cook pasta
according to package instructions.
Rinse in cold water to stop cooking
and drain well. Lay noodles flat,
with plastic wrap between layers to
prevent sticking.

...

In a bowl, stir together remaining
Parmesan, provolone and
mozzarella cheeses.

...

Spread some of the tomato sauce
over the bottom of a 9- x 13-inch
(3 L) baking dish.

...

Arrange a layer of noodles over top
and spoon over more tomato sauce.
Place half of the eggplant slices on
sauce. Cover with one-third of the
shredded cheese mixture. Repeat
with another layer of noodles, sauce
and all of the ricotta mixture. Cover
with more noodles and sauce, and
arrange remaining eggplant over
top. Cover with another one-third of
the shredded cheese mixture. Finish
with a layer of noodles, a layer of
tomato sauce, then the remaining
shredded cheese mixture.

...

Bake in the oven for 45 to
50 minutes or until golden.

VARIATION

Mushroom, Eggplant and Ricotta
Lasagna: Replace half of the
eggplant with 3 or 4 portobello
mushrooms. Slice, then brush with
oil and sprinkle with salt. Broil until
softened.

PASTA FRITTATA

This omelette can be made with any leftover pasta, whether it has tomato sauce,
sausages, peppers or peas. It's ideal with a salad on the side for a quick lunch.

SERVES 1

1 large egg

+ 2 tbsp (30 mL) water

+ 2 tbsp (30 mL) grated Parmesan or
  Pecorino Romano cheese

+ Chopped Italian flat-leaf parsley
  (optional)

+ Salt and freshly ground pepper

+ A little olive oil

+ 1 serving of cooked pasta, at room
  temperature

In a bowl, beat together egg, water,
Parmesan, and parsley (if using).
Season with salt and pepper to
taste.

...

In a small nonstick skillet, heat oil
over medium-high heat. Reheat
pasta in oil. Pour egg mixture over
top. Cook over medium-low heat,
flipping over to finish cooking.

VARIATION

Spicy Pasta Frittata: Add hot pepper
flakes to the skillet along with the
oil.

Dolci

DESSERTS AND OTHER SWEETS

To end the meal on a sweet note, I've chosen flavours inspired by Italy, of course.

FRUIT – Italians prolong the pleasure at the table with perfectly ripe seasonal fruit, simply savouring what nature has to offer. More-elaborate desserts are reserved for celebrations. In this spirit, I've decided to offer you recipes for Campari Citrus Salad and Moscato-Soaked Fruit (see p. 144).

ICE CREAM AND SORBET – In Italy, *la passeggiata* is the tradition of going out after the meal for an ice cream or sorbet and a stroll through town. More than ever before, artisanal ice cream is available here in Canada, so take advantage of this delight while out for a walk or at home. To whet your appetite, you'll find recipes for Mocha-Hazelnut Granita and Chocolate Sorbet (see p. 150), Vanilla Ice Cream with Balsamic Vinegar Strawberries (see p. 146) and Ice Cream Panettone (see p. 148).

COFFEE – Coffee is almost a religion in Italy, and the aroma alone can transport me to the country's narrow streets. Every hour of the day brings a different kind of coffee, and everyone has a favourite way of enjoying it. Its marvelous flavour appears in these pages in the form of a granita, a budino and shortbread.

CHOCOLATE AND NUTS – A simple bowl of nuts for shelling, a square of melt-in-your-mouth dark chocolate or nougat, Chocolate Mascarpone Dip (see p. 146), a slice of Torta Caprese (see p. 161), Mocha Shortbread (see p. 157), biscotti...chocolate and nuts feature prominently in Italian desserts, either alone or combined, as in the unusual chocolate-nut sausage presented in this chapter.

CITRUS – A little taste of sun from southern Italy, lemons and limes are found here in Limoncello (see p. 166), Lime Budino (see p. 164) and Olive Oil and Lemon Loaf (see p. 162).

All this for that final sweet note!

MOSCATO-SOAKED FRUIT

Choose the fruit according to the season and add this aromatic golden elixir.
Grapes are divine, but you can easily replace them with ripe in-season melon,
cantaloupe, peaches, cherries and/or strawberries.

Water
+ Granulated sugar
+ Grapes of 2 or 3 different colours
+ Cold Moscato d'Asti (see p. 185)

In a saucepan, heat equal parts water and sugar until sugar is completely dissolved. Let cool and set aside in the refrigerator.
...

Halve grapes and remove any seeds. Place grapes in a bowl and pour Moscato over top. Sweeten to taste with reserved sugar syrup. Refrigerate for at least 1 hour.
...

Serve in glasses or dessert cups.

CAMPARI CITRUS SALAD

Already a happy pairing, Campari and citrus are sweetened here for a dessert to savour.

SERVES 6 TO 8

1/4 cup (50 mL) water
+ 3 tbsp (45 mL) granulated sugar, or more to taste
+ 1/4 cup (50 mL) Campari (see p. 185)
+ 6 pink grapefruits, or a mix of grapefruits and oranges
+ Pomegranate seeds or snipped fresh mint (optional)

In a small saucepan, heat water and sugar, stirring, until sugar is completely dissolved. Add Campari. Let cool.
...

Holding over a bowl to collect juice, cut peel and pith off grapefruits. Cut segments away from membranes (see p. 170).
...

Stir reserved syrup into juice and fruit segments. Refrigerate for at least 1 hour.
...

Serve chilled. Garnish with pomegranate seeds (if using).

CHOCOLATE MASCARPONE DIP

I like this creamy, chocolaty dip, especially when flavoured with alcohol. Ready in no time, it can be used as a dip for fruit or to ice a cake.

SERVES 6 TO 8

3/4 cup (175 mL) icing sugar

+ 1/4 cup (50 mL) cocoa powder

+ 1 cup (250 mL) mascarpone cheese*, softened

+ 2 to 3 tbsp (30 to 45 mL) amaretto, port or other alcohol (optional)

+ About 1/3 cup (75 mL) milk

*You can substitute cream cheese for the mascarpone.

Sift icing sugar and cocoa together in a bowl.

...

Add mascarpone and beat with an electric mixer or whisk until smooth.

...

Add amaretto (if using). Stir in just enough of the milk to thin to the right consistency for dipping.

TO SERVE

Serve with strawberries, raspberries, cookies or pear wedges.

VANILLA ICE CREAM WITH BALSAMIC VINEGAR STRAWBERRIES

Balsamic vinegar drizzled on vanilla ice cream or strawberries is a familiar tune by now. For this dish, use a good-quality balsamic vinegar, one that is aged and syrupy. For a change, you can substitute vino cotto, a condiment well worth discovering.

Vanilla ice cream

+ Sliced strawberries

+ Aged balsamic vinegar or vino cotto (see p. 183)

+ Snipped fresh basil or freshly ground pepper (optional)

+ Cookies

Top ice cream with strawberries. Drizzle with a thin stream of balsamic vinegar and sprinkle with basil (if using).

...

Serve with cookies.

VARIATIONS

Replace strawberries with mangoes, peaches, fresh figs, blackberries or raspberries.

ICE CREAM PANETTONE

Panettone is a sweet bread that's a favourite during the Christmas holidays.
Whether you use panettone or pandoro (another baked delight), as we have in the photo,
this frozen dessert will be regal and *simplissimo* to prepare.

SERVES 8 TO 10

4 cups (1 L) vanilla ice cream

+ 1 panettone or pandoro (see p. 184)

+ 5 tbsp (75 mL) amaretto, Cointreau
  or rum

+ 1 cup (250 mL) frozen raspberries

+ 1/2 cup (125 mL) toasted slivered
  almonds (see p. 173), or to taste

+ 3 to 4 tbsp (45 to 60 mL) finely grated
  or chopped gingerroot

+ Icing sugar

+ Fruit coulis or chocolate sauce
  (optional)

Place ice cream in the refrigerator for 30 minutes or until just soft enough to be worked.

...

Cut a 1 1/2-inch (4 cm) thick slice off the base of the panettone. Set aside.

...

Using a knife, hollow out panettone, leaving sides about 1 inch (2.5 cm) thick. Brush the inside with amaretto.

...

In a bowl, stir together ice cream, raspberries, almonds and ginger. Spoon mixture into hollowed-out panettone. Replace base and repack panettone in its original wrapping. Freeze for at least 8 hours.

TO SERVE

Place panettone in the refrigerator for 45 minutes before serving. Dust with icing sugar. Cut into wedges and serve with coulis (if using).

NOTE

Use the leftover panettone to make a delicious bread pudding.

VARIATION

Double Ice Cream Panettone: An even more tempting method is to brush the hollowed-out panettone with amaretto, then fill halfway with ice cream. Freeze for at least 30 minutes, then fill with a different flavour of ice cream or sorbet. Replace cake base and freeze.

CHOCOLATE SORBET

This recipe is inspired by a sorbet created by Mark Bittman, food columnist for *The New York Times*. Despite the very rich chocolate flavour, it has the freshness of a sorbet.

SERVES 6

3/4 cup (175 mL) granulated sugar
+ 3/4 cup (175 mL) cocoa powder
+ 2 cups (500 mL) boiling water
+ 1 tsp (5 mL) vanilla extract
+ Crumbled chocolate cookies or berries (optional)

Combine sugar and cocoa powder in a bowl. Stir well. Gradually pour in boiling water, whisking until sugar and cocoa are completely dissolved. Stir in vanilla and let cool.

...

Pour mixture into a 9-inch (23 cm) square dish. Freeze for at least 3 hours or until solid.

...

With a knife, cut into chunks and transfer to food processor. Pulse until smooth, scraping down side of bowl several times with a spatula. Return mixture to pan and freeze for 30 minutes.

TO SERVE

Garnish individual portions with crumbled chocolate cookies (if using).

NOTES

Any leftover sorbet that has frozen solid again can be pulsed in the food processor.

...

You can also prepare the sorbet in an ice cream maker, following the manufacturer's instructions.

MOCHA-HAZELNUT GRANITA

In Naples, many bars offer a variety of mouth-watering hazelnut coffees: hot, iced, with milk or a shot of something stronger. Here is my granita version.

SERVES 4

2 cups (500 mL) hot espresso
+ 1/2 cup (125 mL) chocolate-hazelnut spread, such as Nutella

Combine coffee and hazelnut spread in a glass baking dish. Let cool to room temperature.

...

Freeze for 3 to 4 hours, scratching surface with a fork several times during freezing, until mixture is frozen and grainy.

...

If you do not serve the granita immediately, it may harden into a block. If this happens, break it into chunks and grind it in a food processor before serving.

TO SERVE

You can garnish with whipped cream and top with finely shaved chocolate.

NOTE

You can store this granita in the freezer by transferring it to a freezer bag and removing the air from the bag.

BISCOTTI FOR DIPPING

In Italy, all cookies are called biscotti, not just the long dry ones that we dip into wine, coffee or tea.
Biscotti means "twice baked": first in a long log and second sliced into cookies.
If you add butter, the *biscotti* will be dry, as opposed to very dry. The latter are kept for
dipping into wine such as vino santo (see p. 185) or another sweet wine, ice cider, tea or coffee.
Biscotti keep for ages and make a much-appreciated gift. They do require some skill to make,
but the technique is not unpleasant and the reward is dessert!

MAKES 36 COOKIES

2 tbsp (30 mL) anise seeds

+ 3 tbsp (45 mL) Sambuca, Pernod
  or Ricard liqueur (optional)

+ 2 3/4 cups (675 mL) all-purpose flour*

+ 1 tsp (5 mL) baking powder

+ 1/4 tsp (1 mL) salt

+ 3/4 cup (175 mL) granulated sugar

+ 3 large room-temperature eggs, beaten

+ 2 tsp (10 mL) almond extract

+ 1 tsp (5 mL) vanilla extract

+ 1 cup (250 mL) whole almonds

*You may need more flour if the dough is too sticky.

Preheat oven to 350°F (180°C). Line a baking sheet with parchment paper or a silicone baking mat, or use a nonstick baking sheet.

...

In a small bowl, soak anise seeds in Sambuca (if using).

...

In another bowl, stir together flour, baking powder and salt. Set aside.

...

In a large bowl, using an electric mixer, beat sugar and all but 2 tbsp (30 mL) of the beaten eggs until creamy and pale yellow. Add almond extract, vanilla and anise seeds.

...

Using a wooden spoon or working with your hands if dough is stiff, stir dry ingredients and almonds into egg mixture. Add a little extra flour if the dough is too sticky.

...

Divide dough in half and shape each into a 14-inch (35 cm) long log. Place on prepared baking sheet and flatten to 2 1/2 inches (6 cm) wide.

...

Brush logs with reserved beaten egg.

...

Bake on the middle rack of oven for 20 to 25 minutes or until firm to the touch. Using 2 spatulas, transfer each log to a rack and let cool for about 15 minutes.

...

Reduce oven temperature to 300°F (150°C).

...

Holding logs firmly on a cutting board and using a bread knife, cut diagonally into 3/8-inch (0.9 cm) thick slices.

...

Transfer back to the baking sheet and bake, turning over halfway through, for 15 to 20 minutes or until dry.

...

Transfer to a rack and let cool. Biscotti will keep in a tin for several weeks.

VARIATIONS

Sparkly Biscotti: After brushing biscotti with beaten egg, sprinkle with raw sugar, such as turbinado or Demerara.

...

Softer Biscotti: Beat 1/2 cup (125 mL) butter, softened, with sugar before adding eggs.

DOUBLE CHOCOLATE BISCOTTI

This cookie would go nicely with a scoop of vanilla, pistachio or berry ice cream,
or dipped into a cup of good coffee – black or with a few drops of alcohol.
Slicing the baked log into biscotti is tricky, but the crumbs are delicious.

MAKES 36 COOKIES

2 cups (500 mL) all-purpose flour*

+ 1/2 cup (125 mL) cocoa powder

+ 1 tsp (5 mL) baking soda

+ 1/2 tsp (2 mL) salt

+ 1/4 cup (50 mL) butter, softened

+ 1 cup (250 mL) granulated sugar

+ 2 large room-temperature eggs

+ 2 tsp (10 mL) vanilla extract

+ 2 tsp (10 mL) almond extract

+ 1 cup (250 mL) whole pistachios

+ 5 oz (150 g) dark (58 to 70% cocoa)
  or bittersweet chocolate, chopped or
  in chips

* You may need more flour if the dough is too
sticky.

Preheat oven to 325°F (160°C). Line a baking sheet with parchment paper or a silicone baking mat, or use a nonstick baking sheet.

...

In a bowl, sift together flour, cocoa powder, baking soda and salt. Set aside.

...

In a large bowl, using an electric mixer, beat butter and sugar until well blended. Beat in eggs, 1 at a time, beating until smooth after each addition.

...

Beat in vanilla and almond extracts.

...

Using a wooden spoon or working with your hands if dough is stiff, stir dry ingredients, pistachios and chocolate into butter mixture. Add a little extra flour if the dough is too sticky.

...

Divide dough in half and shape each into a 10-inch (25 cm) long log. Place on prepared baking sheet and flatten to 3 inches (8 cm) wide.

...

Bake on the middle rack of oven for 30 minutes or until firm to the touch. Using 2 spatulas, transfer each log to a rack and let cool for at least 20 minutes.

...

Reduce oven temperature to 300°F (150°C).

...

Holding logs firmly on a cutting board and using a bread knife, cut diagonally into 1/2-inch (1 cm) thick slices.

...

Transfer back to the baking sheet and bake, turning over halfway through, for 20 minutes or until dry.

...

Transfer to a rack and let cool. Biscotti will keep in a tin for about 2 weeks.

VARIATIONS

Sparkly Double Chocolate Biscotti: Before baking, brush logs with beaten egg and sprinkle with raw sugar, such as turbinado or Demerara.

...

Glazed Double Chocolate Biscotti: Glaze cooled biscotti partially with melted chocolate.

MOCHA-CASHEW BISCOTTI

There is nothing traditional about these coffee, cashew and chocolate biscotti except their shape – and their popularity!

MAKES 36 COOKIES

2 1/2 cups (625 mL) all-purpose flour*
+ 1 tsp (5 mL) baking powder
+ 1/4 tsp (1 mL) salt
+ 1/2 cup (125 mL) butter, softened
+ 1 cup (250 mL) packed brown sugar or granulated sugar
+ 2 large room-temperature eggs
+ 2 tbsp (30 mL) instant coffee, dissolved in 1 tbsp (15 mL) boiling water
+ 1 tsp (5 mL) vanilla extract
+ 1 1/4 cups (300 mL) raw cashews or pecans
+ 1/2 cup (125 mL) bittersweet chocolate chips or chopped dark (70% cocoa) chocolate
+ 1 large egg, beaten

*You may need more flour if the dough is too sticky.

Preheat oven to 350°F (180°C). Line a baking sheet with parchment paper or a silicone baking mat, or use a nonstick baking sheet.

...

In a bowl, stir together flour, baking powder and salt. Set aside.

...

In a large bowl, using an electric mixer, beat butter and brown sugar until well blended. Beat in eggs, 1 at a time, beating until smooth after each addition. Beat in coffee and vanilla.

...

Using a wooden spoon or your hands if the dough is stiff, stir dry ingredients, cashews and chocolate chips into butter mixture. Add a little extra flour if the dough is too sticky.

...

Divide dough in half and shape each into a 14-inch (35 cm) long log. Place on prepared baking sheet and flatten to 2 1/2 inches (6 cm) wide. Brush logs with beaten egg.

...

Bake on the middle rack of oven for 20 to 25 minutes or until firm to the touch. Using 2 spatulas, transfer each log to a rack and let cool for about 15 minutes.

...

Reduce oven temperature to 300°F (150°C).

...

Holding logs firmly on a cutting board and using a bread knife, cut diagonally into 1/2-inch (1 cm) thick slices.

...

Transfer back to the baking sheet and bake, turning over halfway through, for 15 to 20 minutes or until dry.

...

Transfer to a rack and let cool. Biscotti will keep in a tin for about 2 weeks.

VARIATION

Sparkly Mocha-Cashew Biscotti: After brushing logs with beaten egg, sprinkle with raw sugar, such as turbinado or Demerara.

MOCHA SHORTBREAD

These heavenly melt-in-your-mouth shortbreads can be frozen in logs and baked whenever you like.
It's a little bliss within reach at all times!

MAKES 4 TO 5 DOZEN COOKIES

1 1/2 cups (375 mL) all-purpose flour

+ 1/2 cup (125 mL) cocoa powder

+ 1/4 tsp (1 mL) salt

+ 1 cup (250 mL) butter, softened

+ 3/4 cup (175 mL) + 2 tbsp (30 mL) icing sugar

+ 1/3 cup (75 mL) cornstarch

+ 1 tbsp (15 mL) instant coffee

+ Raw sugar, such as Demerara or turbinado (optional)

In a bowl, sift together flour, cocoa powder and salt. Set aside.

...

In a large bowl, using an electric mixer, beat butter for 30 seconds. Add icing sugar and cornstarch and beat for 5 minutes or until creamy and well blended. Stir in coffee.

...

Beat in dry ingredients on low speed until smooth dough forms. Work ingredients in with hands if dough is stiff.

...

Divide dough in half and shape each into a 1 1/2-inch (4 cm) diameter log. Wrap logs separately in plastic wrap and refrigerate for 2 hours.

...

Roll logs in raw sugar (if using). Slice into 1/4-inch (5 mm) thick rounds.

...

Preheat oven to 325°F (160°C).

...

Line a baking sheet with parchment paper or a silicone baking mat, or use a nonstick baking sheet. Arrange cookies on prepared baking sheet, spacing 3/4 inch (2 cm) apart.

...

Bake on the middle rack of oven for 8 to 10 minutes.

...

Let cool slightly before handling. Transfer to a rack and let cool completely. Store in a tin for up to 2 weeks.

VARIATION

Spicy Cinnamon Shortbread: Replace coffee with 1 to 2 tsp (5 to 10 mL) cinnamon and 1/8 to 1/4 tsp (0.5 to 1 mL) cayenne pepper, adding both to the flour mixture.

CHOCOLATE-FIG SAUSAGE

Chocolate, dried figs and nuts make an exquisite combination. In Italy, these funny dried-fruit-and-nut "sausages" are found in fine food stores. They're nibbled for dessert or make a pretty gift when wrapped in parchment paper and tied with a ribbon – or even butcher paper and string.

MAKES 30 SLICES

4 oz (125 g) bittersweet or dark (70% cocoa) chocolate

+ 3 tbsp (45 mL) butter
+ 1 to 1 1/2 cups (250 to 375 mL) chopped dried figs
+ 1 cup (250 mL) coarsely chopped toasted pistachios, hazelnuts or almonds (see p. 173)
+ 1 cup (250 mL) crisp rice cereal, such as Rice Krispies
+ 2 tbsp (30 mL) icing sugar

Melt chocolate and butter together in a double boiler or the microwave.

...

In a bowl, mix together figs, pistachios, rice cereal and melted chocolate.

...

Divide mixture in half, placing each half on a large piece of plastic wrap. Shape each into a 2-inch (5 cm) diameter log measuring at least 7 inches (18 cm) long. Wrap sausages tightly, pressing firmly to prevent them from crumbling when cut.

...

Refrigerate for 3 to 4 hours.

...

Unwrap sausages and, 1 at a time, place in a plastic bag with icing sugar. Shake to coat well. For a more realistic effect, wrap with string to look like a deli sausage and place on a wooden board.

TO SERVE

Cut into 3/8-inch (0.9 cm) thick slices with a bread knife.

TORTA CAPRESE

There are many versions of this flourless, very dense chocolate cake that originated on the Italian island of Capri. I tried this version from Edda Bini Mastropasqua during a delightful visit to the neighbouring island of Ischia. Thank you, Edda, for sharing your delectable family recipe with me!

SERVES 12 TO 15

7 oz (200 g) dark (70% cocoa) or bittersweet chocolate, chopped
+ 1 cup (250 mL) butter
+ 1/4 cup (50 mL) brewed espresso or strong coffee
+ 1 2/3 cups (400 mL) whole almonds or 2 cups (500 mL) ground almonds
+ 1 tbsp (15 mL) baking powder
+ 1 cup (250 mL) granulated sugar
+ 5 large room-temperature eggs
+ Cocoa powder or icing sugar

Preheat oven to 350°F (180°C). Butter and flour a 10-inch (25 cm) springform pan or pie plate.

...

Melt chocolate and butter together in a double boiler or the microwave. Stir in espresso and let cool to room temperature.

...

If using whole almonds, grind them in a small food processor or coffee grinder.

...

In a bowl, combine ground almonds and baking powder. Set aside.

...

In a large bowl, using an electric mixer, beat sugar and eggs at high speed for 5 minutes or until batter is creamy and pale yellow. Stir in almond mixture.

...

Gently stir in chocolate mixture. Pour batter into prepared pan.

...

Bake on the middle rack of oven for 40 minutes or until centre is firm to the touch. Transfer pan to a rack and let cool. The cake will become firmer as it cools.

TO SERVE

Let cake cool for at least 4 hours before transferring to a serving plate. If you like, dust with cocoa powder or icing sugar just before serving.

OLIVE OIL AND LEMON LOAF

You may be surprised to find olive oil among the ingredients for a dessert.
You'll likely try this recipe out of curiosity, then make it again for the taste!
Enjoy the loaf on its own or with fruit salad, sorbet, or ice cream and berries.

SERVES 10

LOAF

1 1/2 cups (375 mL) all-purpose flour

+ 1 1/2 tsp (7 mL) baking powder

+ 1/2 tsp (2 mL) salt

+ 4 large room-temperature eggs

+ 3/4 cup (175 mL) granulated sugar

+ 3 to 4 tbsp (45 to 60 mL) finely chopped fresh rosemary (optional)

+ 2 tbsp (30 mL) finely grated lemon or lime rind (organic if possible)

+ 2/3 cup (150 mL) olive oil or butter, softened

+ Rosemary sprigs (optional)

+ Thin lemon slices (optional)

SYRUP

1/3 cup (75 mL) granulated sugar

+ 1/4 cup (50 mL) lemon or lime juice

LOAF

Preheat oven to 350°F (180°C). Oil a 9- x 5-inch (1.5 L) loaf pan.*

...

In a bowl, stir together flour, baking powder and salt. Set aside.

...

In a large bowl, using an electric mixer, beat eggs and sugar at high speed for 3 to 5 minutes or until batter is frothy and pale yellow. Add rosemary (if using) and lemon rind. Continue beating at medium speed, gradually incorporating oil.

...

Add dry ingredients and mix well. Pour batter into prepared pan.

...

Bake on the middle rack of oven for 50 to 60 minutes or until loaf is golden. Check doneness by inserting a toothpick into the centre of the loaf. It should come out clean.

*You can use three 3- x 7-inch (750 mL) loaf pans instead. Reduce baking time to 30 to 35 minutes.

SYRUP

Meanwhile, in a saucepan over medium heat, dissolve sugar in lemon juice.

...

While loaf is still hot, prick top all over with a fork. Gently brush loaf with syrup. Let cool completely before removing from pan.

TO SERVE

Garnish loaf with rosemary sprigs and lemon slices (if using). You can sugar-frost the rosemary first by dipping it in lightly beaten egg white, shaking off excess, then sprinkling with sugar.

LIME BUDINO

A budino is simply a lightly set custard-style pudding. You may think you don't have enough time to make dessert, but you can likely find the few minutes you'll need to make this one.

SERVES 4

2 large room-temperature eggs
+ 1/3 cup (75 mL) granulated sugar
+ 1 cup (250 mL) 15% cream
+ 4 to 5 tbsp (60 to 75 mL) lime juice
+ Your choice of garnish:
    – 2 tbsp (30 mL) finely grated lime rind
    – blueberries or raspberries

Preheat oven to 350°F (180°C).

...

In a bowl, using an electric mixer, beat eggs and sugar at medium speed. Add cream and lime juice, mixing well.

...

Divide mixture among four 3/4-cup (175 mL) ramekins. Place in a roasting pan or 9-inch (23 cm) square baking dish; add boiling water to pan to reach halfway up sides of ramekins.

...

Bake on the middle rack of oven for 20 to 25 minutes. The budino will not be set in the middle.

...

Transfer ramekins to a rack and let cool to room temperature. Refrigerate for at least 2 hours or until chilled.

...

Garnish with your choice of garnish.

VARIATION

Coffee Budino: Replace lime juice with 5 to 6 tbsp (75 to 90 mL) cooled brewed espresso or strong coffee. Garnish with chocolate-covered coffee beans or grated chocolate.

LIMONCELLO

For some Italians, the drink that I've included here is definitely not the traditional recipe, because a good limoncello is made with strong alcohol and, most importantly, lemons picked in Italy. No matter what you call it, this lemon-flavoured vodka is sure to please.

MAKES 6 CUPS (1.5 L)

6 to 8 organic lemons
+ One 750 mL bottle vodka
+ 3 cups (750 mL) water
+ 1 cup (250 mL) granulated sugar

Using a vegetable peeler, remove yellow rind, but not white pith, from the lemons.

...

Place rind in an airtight jar and pour in vodka. Seal and let macerate at room temperature for about 10 days or until rind has flavoured the vodka.

...

Bring water and sugar to a boil in a saucepan and boil for 3 minutes or until sugar is completely dissolved.

...

Strain vodka through a sieve placed over a bowl. Place sieve with lemon peel over a second bowl and pour hot syrup over rind to extract all flavour. Let cool.

...

Add at least 2 cups (500 mL) of the syrup to vodka. Taste and sweeten with more syrup if desired. Use any leftover syrup to flavour fruit salads, iced tea or lemonade.

...

Stir well before pouring. Limoncello will keep for months in the fridge.

TO SERVE

Serve in small glasses that have been frosted in the freezer. Limoncello is perfect in cocktails made with cranberry juice or mixed with sparkling water.

VARIATION

Strong Limoncello: For a version that packs a punch, replace vodka with the same amount of 190-proof alcohol.

LEMON SORBET AND LIMONCELLO

Lemon sorbet
+ Blueberries
+ Limoncello

Place sorbet in frosted dessert cups or glasses. Garnish with blueberries and drizzle with limoncello.

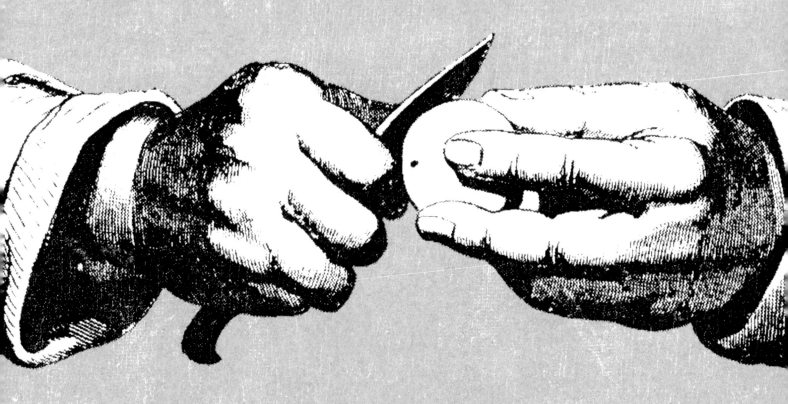

THE BASICS

RECIPES AND TIPS

CITRUS FRUIT

ZESTING

Ideally, you should use organically grown citrus fruit for zest, because there are no trace chemicals or pesticides on the rind. If you do not use organic, wash fruit well by scrubbing under cold running water. For finely grated rind, use a fine grater and work over a bowl or pan to collect all the essential oils in the peel. Do not grate any of the white pith, which is bitter. You can also obtain zest by peeling off, then finely chopping the rind with a chef's knife.

...

EXTRACTING JUICE

A room-temperature fruit yields much more juice than a cold fruit. Roll the fruit firmly on the work surface, pushing down to lightly crush the flesh inside and make the juice easier to extract.

...

REMOVING SEGMENTS

Using a sharp knife, cut ends off fruit. Carve off the peel and all the white pith, leaving as much of the flesh as possible. To remove the segments, slide the knife along the membranes, separating them, and gently cut out each section. Work over a bowl to collect the juice.

GARLIC

SELECTING

For juicier, more flavourful garlic, choose a bulb that is firm to the touch, a sign of freshness. The peel should be intact and completely cover the bulb. There should not be any sign of sprouting.

...

PEELING

To peel a clove of garlic, crush it with a chef's knife, pushing down on the flat of the blade with the heel of your hand. Remove peel, cut clove in half and remove germ if necessary. Chop finely with a very sharp chef's knife or crush in a garlic press.

...

OVEN-ROASTED GARLIC

Roasted garlic has a milder flavour than raw garlic and is much easier to digest.

...

To roast, cut a thin slice off the tip of the garlic bulb, exposing the tops of the cloves. Place bulb on a large square of foil and brush generously with olive oil. Wrap foil around bulb to make an airtight envelope. Bake on the middle rack of preheated 350°F (180°C) oven for about 45 minutes or until fragrant and cloves are soft. Press bulb to squeeze out roasted garlic cloves and mash if desired. Roasted garlic will keep for several days in the refrigerator if covered with a layer of oil in an airtight container. This oil can be used for cooking or in pasta dishes and salads.

ASPARAGUS

STORING

To keep asparagus fresh before using, trim the stalks and place upright in a jar half-full of fresh water. Cover with a plastic bag and store in the refrigerator.

...

TRIMMING AND COOKING

To trim asparagus, break the stalk by bending it back until it snaps. If the stalks are thick, peel with a vegetable peeler to remove exterior fibres, stopping 1 1/2 inches (4 cm) from the tip. If the stalks are slender, they do not need to be peeled.

...

Blanch asparagus in boiling salted water, uncovered, until tender but still slightly crisp. You can also steam it. To roast asparagus in the oven, place on a baking sheet, coat with oil and season with salt. Roast in preheated 425°F (220°C) oven, shaking baking sheet halfway through cooking, for 10 to 15 minutes or until tender-crisp.

EGGPLANT

ROASTING

Wash eggplants and cut off ends. Slice into rounds about 3/8 inch (0.9 cm) thick. If the eggplants are small, slice them lengthwise. Place on a baking sheet and brush both sides with olive oil. Season with salt. Broil for 4 to 5 minutes per side. Watch closely, removing slices as they turn golden.

CHICKEN STOCK

HOMEMADE STOCK

The smell of stock simmering in the house is so comforting! Making your own stock is not really difficult. You simply place all the ingredients in a pot and wait until it is done. There are two little tricks that make a difference, however: make sure the stock barely simmers as it cooks, and skim off any foam.

...

3 lb (1.5 kg) chicken carcasses* and bones, fat removed
+ 1 onion (unpeeled), cut in chunks
+ 1 leek, cut in chunks
+ 2 stalks celery (with leaves), coarsely chopped
+ 2 carrots, peeled and coarsely chopped
+ 2 or 3 plum tomatoes, quartered (optional)
+ 3 or 4 cloves garlic, crushed
+ 1 large bunch Italian flat-leaf parsley
+ 1 bay leaf
+ A few sprigs of thyme or 2 or 3 pinches dried thyme
+ 10 black peppercorns, or to taste
+ Sea salt
+ Other seasonings you can add: sprigs of fresh herbs, the skins from peeled tomatoes, fennel stalks and the tough green part of leeks (optional)

*You can also use the wings, drumsticks and neck.

...

Rinse carcasses and bones under cold running water. In a large stock pot, combine carcasses, bones, onion, leek, celery, carrots, tomatoes (if using), garlic, parsley, bay leaf, thyme, peppercorns, salt and other seasonings (if using). Add enough water to cover by about 1 1/2 inches (4 cm). Bring to a boil, skimming off any foam that forms on the surface with a slotted spoon.

...

Simmer over low heat, uncovered, for 1 1/2 hours. Be sure to keep the simmer very gentle. Strain stock. To remove fat, let stock cool in the refrigerator overnight, then lift the solidified fat off the surface.

...

Freeze the stock in resealable freezer bags and/or airtight containers and use within 3 months. Before adding stock to a recipe, taste and add salt if necessary.

FENNEL

TRIMMING
Cut off the stalks, reserving to make vegetable or meat stock. Peel off the outermost leaves if bruised. Cut bulb in half, then into wedges, but do not core; leave the innermost layers attached to one another by the core.

FRESH HERBS

STORING
Place herbs between two moist paper towels in an airtight container and store in the refrigerator.

...

PREPARING
To remove the leaves from woody-stemmed herbs, such as thyme and rosemary, hold the stem in one hand and slide the thumb and index finger of your other hand along the stem to strip off the leaves.

...

For tender herbs, such as parsley, basil, dill, oregano, coriander and mint, pick the leaves off the stems by hand. Chop them with a very sharp chef's knife or mezzaluna. To snip herbs, use scissors or a chef's knife.

...

To measure chopped herbs or whole leaves, pack into the measuring spoon or cup.

NUTS (WALNUTS, HAZELNUTS, ALMONDS, PECANS AND OTHERS)

SELECTING AND STORING
Purchase nuts at a store with high turnover; the fresher the nuts, the better they'll taste. Store in the fridge or freezer in airtight containers.

...

TOASTING
Place nuts on a baking sheet and toast in a preheated 350°F (180°C) oven for 8 to 10 minutes (walnuts, hazelnuts, whole almonds and pecans), 5 to 7 minutes (pistachios) or 4 to 5 minutes (slivered almonds, pine nuts). Check nuts regularly and remove once they are light golden.

OLIVES

PITTING
Place olives in a plastic bag and crush with the bottom of a small saucepan or can. Or use a chef's knife, smashing them under the side of the blade with the heel of your hand, then removing pits. An olive pitter is another option, and it leaves a neater result.

FRESH PASTA

My friend Elena Faita, a wonderful cook and owner of Montreal's well-known Dante Hardware cooking store, always sings the praises of fresh pasta to me, but I'm a dry pasta girl myself. For Elena, who created this recipe, kneading and shaping the dough is second nature – a game, even, which involves making something from nothing, since all you need is flour and water. Then, as if by magic, the pasta ends up on your dinner plate.

MAKING YOUR OWN PASTA
SERVES 4 / MAKES 1 LB (500 G)

3 cups (750 mL) unbleached flour or Italian 00 flour*

+ 4 large room-temperature eggs

+ 2 tbsp (30 mL) olive oil

+ 2 to 3 tbsp (30 to 45 mL) water, if necessary

*Italian 00 flour is ultra finely milled and is often recommended for making pasta.

Preparing the dough by hand

Sift flour into a mound on the work surface.

...

Make a deep 6- to 8-inch (15 to 20 cm) wide well in the middle of the flour. Add eggs and oil to well.

...

With a fork, stir eggs using a circular motion, gradually incorporating flour. Be careful not to break the well wall or the eggs will spill onto the work surface. To prevent this, constantly press the outer edge of the well toward the centre.

...

As soon as the dough is too stiff for the fork, continue working with your fingers. Incorporate as much flour as the dough can absorb. You have enough flour when dry lumps begin to fall off the ball of dough. Too much flour is worse than not enough, since you can always add more while kneading.

...

Set the dough aside and clean the work surface with a metal spatula.

...

Lightly flour work surface. Flatten the ball of dough and knead from the middle away from you with the heel of your hand. Fold dough in half, rotate 180 degrees and knead again, repeating for about 10 minutes or until dough is smooth, elastic and silky. The dough should no longer stick to the work surface and should spring back to its original shape when pressed.

...

Place dough in a bowl and cover. Let rest for 10 to 30 minutes at room temperature.

...

Preparing the dough in a food processor

Use the dough blade. Place flour, eggs and oil in the food processor. Pulse, gradually adding water, until a ball forms. Knead for 10 minutes as described above.

...

Rolling out with a pasta maker

To roll out dough, you'll need a large work surface and several dry, clean dish towels.

...

Cut dough into 8 to 10 pieces. Wrap in a towel and set aside.

...

Flatten 1 piece of dough between your hands into a flat disc about 3/8 inch (0.9 cm) thick. Position pasta machine rollers at their widest setting and roll disc through opening. Fold pasta in half and roll again at the same setting.

...

Set aside strip of dough on a dish towel.

...

Repeat with remaining pieces of dough, setting the rolled strips side-by-side on towels without letting them touch.

...

Reduce roller width by 1 notch and roll each strip of dough through again. Continue, reducing width of space between rollers each time until pasta is the desired thickness.

...

Cut pasta sheets into desired shapes.

...

HERB PASTA

Roll dough and top with Italian flat-leaf parsley or sage leaves. Fold dough over and roll through pasta maker again, or roll into a single sheet by hand using a rolling pin. This is a great way to add herbs to larger shaped pasta, such as lasagna and pappardelle, which can later be hand-cut with a knife.

...

COOKING FRESH PASTA

The cooking time depends on the thickness of the pasta. Cook thin machine-cut pasta for 30 seconds to 1 minute. Adjust the cooking time upward for thicker or hand-shaped pasta. Test for doneness before draining!

PARMESAN CHEESE

SELECTING AND STORING

Purchase a piece of Parmesan that you can grate at home as you need it. You can keep the rinds and pop them into a pot of soup, stew (osso bucco, for example) or tomato sauce near the end of cooking to enhance the flavour of the dish. Store Parmesan cheese the same way as you would any ripened cheese: wrap in parchment or waxed paper, then overwrap with foil. Definitely do not store cheese in the torn original packaging or plastic wrap.

...

SHAVINGS

To make Parmesan or grana Padano shavings, the cheese should be at room temperature. Using a peeler on the smooth side of the cheese, press downward in a single motion until the cheese curls as the blade cuts through it. Shavings are easiest to make with a young Parmesan or grana Padano, because it is not as dry and thus less likely to crumble.

GREEN PEAS

Fresh greens peas are hard to come by and fragile. To prevent them from becoming starchy, keep them in their pods for no longer than 12 hours. Once they're shelled, you should refrigerate and consume them without delay. Cook them as little as possible to keep their colour and flavour.

...

You can take advantage of the colour this vegetable brings to any plate by using frozen green peas. You'll be pleasantly surprised by the quality.

SWEET PEPPERS

ROASTING AND PEELING

Wash and dry the peppers. Place on a baking sheet and brush with olive oil. Roast in preheated 400°F (200°C) oven for about 30 minutes, turning once or twice. The peppers will soften, darken and sag slightly. Transfer from the oven to a bowl and cover with a lid or plate. The resulting steam and condensation will loosen the skin, making the peppers easier to peel. Let cool; remove stems, cut peppers in half, seed and peel. You can roast peppers ahead of time and store them in the fridge for 2 to 3 days.

PROSCIUTTO

SELECTING

Buy prosciutto from a butcher, who will slice it to the thickness you desire. Eat it that very day; it will be more flavourful and the texture better than any sliced vacuum-packed prosciutto you can buy.

RAPINI

SELECTING AND PREPARING

Select a bunch that is bright green with no wilted leaves. Cut off the bottom 1/2 inch (1 cm) of the stalks and remove any bruised leaves. To blanch, plunge into boiling generously salted water for 1 minute. Drain and immediately rinse under cold running water. The rapini will then be ready for pan-frying or for use in a recipe.

TOMATOES

If tomatoes are going into a dish that will be cooked, you should, ideally, peel and seed them first.
...

PEELING

Cut an X in the base of each tomato. Plunge tomatoes into boiling water for 10 to 15 seconds or until skin begins to loosen. Immediately plunge into very cold or ice water for about 30 seconds to stop them from cooking further. Remove skin and stem with a knife.
...

SEEDING

Cut tomatoes in half horizontally and gently press with your fingers or a spoon to squeeze out juice and seeds.

ROASTED TOMATOES

These tomatoes are wonderful for bruschetta or in a pasta dish.

1 package cherry or grape tomatoes
+ A little olive oil
+ Salt

Place tomatoes on a baking sheet and coat generously with oil. Roast in a preheated 450°F (230°C) oven for 10 minutes. Season with salt to taste.

OIL-PACKED SUN-DRIED TOMATOES

Dry-packed sun-dried tomatoes can be rehydrated and placed in a jar with oil. To do so, cover the tomatoes with boiling water and let soak for 20 minutes or until tender. Pat dry thoroughly with a paper towel. Place in a jar and cover with good olive oil. You can flavour the tomatoes with herbs or spices if you like. Store in the refrigerator.

GLOSSARY

CHEESES

ASIAGO, CROTONESE AND PECORINO ROMANO

Pecorino Romano is often called simply Romano. When fairly aged and thus dry, these cheeses are grated and added to pasta dishes at the last minute. You can also serve them at the end of the meal; just be sure to take them out of the fridge one hour beforehand. They'll be excellent accompanied by dried fruit and toasted nuts.

...

CACIOCAVALLO, FONTINA AND PROVOLONE

These are three pressed Italian cheeses that can replace firm mozzarella in a gratin, on pizza or in a panini.

...

GORGONZOLA AND TORTA

Two blue cheeses with very creamy textures, they're good on a stick of celery or an endive spear and give lots of flavour and creaminess to pasta dishes and polenta. Torta is a mixture of Gorgonzola and mascarpone. These cheeses are greatly appreciated to wind up a meal.

...

GRANA PADANO

Grana is the generic name for a type of firm, granular cheese. The best known are grana Padano and Parmigiano-Reggiano (see Parmesan, right). An excellent grating cheese, grana Padano makes a less-expensive substitute for Parmigiano-Reggiano. Grate older cheeses and use younger ones to make shavings, since they will be less crumbly and thus more satisfying.

...

MASCARPONE

This fresh, creamy-textured, smooth cheese became popular thanks to tiramisu and is favoured in desserts above all. You can flavour it with honey, citrus zest or spices. Mascarpone is used in savoury dishes, too, and goes well with pasta.

...

MOZZARELLA DI BUFALA, FIOR DI LATTE, MOZZARINA, FIRM MOZZARELLA AND BOCCONCINI

All of these cheeses are pressed pulled-curd cheeses that suit pasta dishes, pizzas, paninis, salads and a wide range of other dishes.

...

Mozzarella di bufala is imported from Italy. A fresh (unripened) cheese, it is made from water buffalo milk. Fior di latte is a fresh mozzarella, another Italian import, made from cow's milk. The Canadian version is called mozzarina and is produced in Quebec.

...

Firm mozzarella made from cow's milk is a briefly aged cheese that can be grated. It is found mainly in North America.

...

Bocconcini are the siblings of fresh mozzarella. Barely salted, these small balls of cheese require considerable seasoning with fresh herbs, pesto and olive oil.

...

PARMESAN

What can I say about this uniquely flavoured cheese? Parmesan that has the controlled-origin label "Parmigiano-Reggiano" comes from specific areas within the Emilia-Romagna region of Italy. This raw cow's milk cheese is aged for 12, 24 or 36 months or even longer, the dryness and flavour of the cheese increasing with age. A Parmesan cut into bites and served alone or with a good aged balsamic vinegar makes a nice start or end to a meal.

...

RICOTTA AND RICOTTA SALATA

Here in Canada, fresh ricotta is made from cow's milk. This very mild cheese suits sweet or savoury dishes equally well. You'll find the fresh version in Italian grocery stores or regular supermarkets. Add 2 or 3 tbsp (30 or 45 mL) cream to each cup (250 mL) fresh ricotta and use this mixture in gratins, pasta dishes or stuffings. Ricotta can also be spread on toast for breakfast.

...

Ricotta salata is a ripened sheep's milk cheese that has a pleasantly strong, salty taste. A firm and somewhat granular cheese, it is ideal for grating over pasta or risotto, or for eating after a meal.

CONDIMENTS, ETC.

ANCHOVIES

These small boneless fish fillets are preserved in salt or olive oil. Since anchovies are very salty, you might want to rinse and pat them dry before using. Anchovy paste makes a very practical alternative. This purée of anchovies and olive oil is sold in tubes in fine and specialty food shops.

...

BALSAMIC VINEGAR

This vinegar is made from the must (the juicy pulp left after grapes are pressed) of cooked white grapes. Old vinegar is added to start the fermentation process, and the resulting new balsamic vinegar is then aged in wooden casks in the same way as wine. You can find balsamic vinegars that have been aged for eight, 12 or even 25 or more years (this last type is called *extra vecchio*).

...

The older the vinegar, the more concentrated, syrupy and sweet it will be. The acidity also declines with age, but the price goes up! Use the youngest vinegars in salads and marinades, and enjoy the oldest drizzled on meat (veal or beef), grilled fish or vegetables, a bite of Parmesan, fruit (strawberries, peaches and pears), pasta, risotto, carpaccio and even vanilla ice cream.

...

Ideally, whether you choose a young or old vinegar, it should be labelled *aceto balsamico tradizionale di Modena* or *aceto balsamico tradizionale di Reggio Emilia,* which attests to its quality.

...

CAPERS

Made from the flower buds of the caper bush, this little condiment is packed in salt, vinegar or olive oil. Capers preserved in brine or salt should be rinsed before using. Simply soak in cold water and pat dry.

...

DRIED PORCINI

Known as porcini in Italy, these mushrooms are sometimes called ceps or boletus elsewhere. No matter what they're called, they are among the most flavourful, especially when dried. A culinary lifesaver, they boost the flavour of risottos, pasta dishes and sauces. Porcini will keep for more than a year if you store them in an airtight container in a dry, cool spot.

...

EXTRA-VIRGIN OLIVE OIL

Fruity, spicy or peppery extra-virgin (first-press) olive oil is the best available. Produced without any chemicals or additives, this oil is very high in antioxidants. You should keep several varieties of olive oil on hand to suit your cooking needs. Use the very best as a dip for chunks of artisanal bread or for flavouring grilled fish or vegetables, pasta or gourmet salad greens.

...

The colour of the oil can range from green to gold but is no gauge of quality. Some high-quality oils may turn cloudy if they haven't been filtered, so don't judge by appearance. Look for a first-press, extra-virgin olive oil with less than 1% acidity. The degree of oleic acidity is normally marked on the label or stamped directly on the bottle. To prevent olive oils from going rancid, store them in a cool place away from light.

...

FRESH AND DRIED CHILI PEPPERS

Since every variety of dried or fresh pepper has its own flavour and degree of heat, use them sparingly. You can always increase the amount, which is preferable to burning your taste buds! If they're in season, opt for fresh chili peppers. Otherwise, dried peppers and hot pepper flakes are fine.

...

PINE NUTS

Pine nuts come from different varieties of pine trees. Italy is a major producer and has been a major consumer for a long time. Buy pine nuts in small quantities and store them in an airtight container in the fridge or freezer. You should do the same with all nuts to keep them from going rancid.

...

VINO COTTO

Vino cotto is simply grape must that is gently cooked to yield a sweet-tasting concentrated syrup. The name varies depending on the origin: it's sometimes called *mosto cotto, saba* or *sapa*. You can use vino cotto to flavour sauces, fruit and desserts. Often used to set off the flavours of a dish, it can be drizzled around a salad, grilled vegetables or many other foods.

...

WHITE BALSAMIC VINEGAR

Considered a condiment rather than a vinegar, this should really be called "balsamic-style" white vinegar, because the production method differs from that of balsamic vinegar and it is not aged in casks. Ranging from clear to amber in hue, white balsamic vinegar tastes similar to cider vinegar, with a very fruity finish. It can replace traditional balsamic vinegar on fish, poultry, pork, veal, salads and fruit.

CURED MEATS

BRESAOLA AND GRISONS BEEF
These two specialty meats are both produced from beef thigh. Bresaola is Italian in origin, and Grisons (also called *Bündnerfleisch*) comes from the French name for the Swiss canton of Graubünden. In both cases, the meat is salted, then dried for several months, resulting in fairly lean meat that should be finely sliced to be fully appreciated.
...

GUANCIALE
This cured meat is made from pig's jowl. Very similar to bacon and pancetta, guanciale is salted but not smoked. If you have trouble finding it, you can substitute pancetta.
...

PANCETTA
Pancetta is made from pork breast (flank). Often rolled like a large salami, it resembles bacon but is not always smoked. Different varieties, such as smoked, spiced and herbed, are available. You can replace it with bacon.
...

PROSCIUTTO
This raw ham is made from pork thigh that is boned, salted, then simply aged and dried. You can find prosciutto imported from Italy in fine food stores and Italian grocery stores.
...

SPECK
This is another type of raw ham made from pork thigh. Unlike prosciutto, speck is lightly smoked. After the bone is removed, the meat is salted, seasoned (with garlic, herbs and spices) and lightly smoked before being aged and dried. It's a specialty of Italy's Trentino–South Tyrol region and can be replaced by traditional prosciutto.

SWEETS

BISCOTTI
Irresistible! These cookies are called biscotti ("twice baked") because they're baked in a log first, then sliced for a second baking. Traditionally, biscotti are quite dry, making them nice to dip in vino santo, coffee and other beverages.
...

PANETTONE AND PANDORO
These traditional sweet yeast breads are served during the Christmas holidays. Panettone is a specialty of Milan, and the star-shaped pandoro originated in Venice. Simple and light, they are available plain or with candied fruit or chocolate. Serve them sliced and toasted for breakfast, as an afternoon snack with a glass of Moscato or at the end of a meal. Panettone also makes delicious French toast.
...

PANFORTE
A type of unleavened flat cake, panforte is made from dried fruit, candied fruit and nuts. Flavoured with honey and spices, this specialty of Sienna is very tasty.

TOMATOES

PLUM TOMATOES
A very common ingredient in Italian cuisine, the tomato actually comes from the Americas. When they're in season, choose Romanello, Roma or San Marzano varieties and take advantage of their availability to make a sauce, or simply peel and can or freeze them. You'll be glad you stocked up come winter!
...

SUN-DRIED TOMATOES
Sun-dried tomatoes are fragrant and slightly sweet. To rehydrate dry-packed ones, place in oil before using (see p. 179). You can also buy them already packed in oil and ready to use. They add flavour to pasta dishes, crostini or salads.
...

TOMATO CONCENTRATE
Sold in tubes, this tomato paste is available in different strengths; it may be labelled double or triple concentrated (*doppio* or *triplo concentrato*). You can find it in Italian grocery stores and, increasingly, in regular supermarkets. Tomato concentrate is made from ripe, sun-drenched tomatoes – a difference you can taste. The advantage of this product is that an open tube will keep for a very long time in the fridge without oxidizing or changing.
...

TOMATO PASTE
Tomato paste is sold in cans. You can freeze any leftover paste in an ice cube tray. To store it in the fridge, cover with a layer of olive oil.

WINE AND SPIRITS

AMARETTO

This almond-flavoured liqueur originated in the 16th century. It is made from bitter almonds (and/or drupe fruit pits, such as from apricots), which give it its name – the root is the Italian word *amaro*, meaning "bitter." Amaretto is a popular cocktail ingredient but is also used in the kitchen to make desserts; in particular, to flavour cookies, cakes, vanilla ice cream, coffee, etc.

...

CAMPARI

A red alcoholic drink with a rather bitter flavour, Campari is made from an infusion of herbs, fruit and other ingredients. It is often combined with orange juice and served over ice or cut with sparkling water.

...

GRAPPA

The ultimate Italian eau-de-vie, grappa is made from grape pomace, or the skins, seeds and stems left over after the grapes have been pressed. It is about 40% alcohol, or 80 proof, and is served at the end of a meal. A young grappa is clear and should be consumed cold, at around 50°F (10°C); older grappa is amber and should be drunk at around 61°F (16°C).

...

LIMONCELLO

This liqueur is made from lemons, and not just any lemons – they must come from the south of Italy. Limoncello is served very cold as a digestif. You can also drizzle it over lemon sorbet or vanilla ice cream to make *sgroppino*. Include it in cocktails made with cranberry juice, sparkling water or sparkling wine.

...

MOSCATO D'ASTI

A fruity, very aromatic white wine, Moscato d'Asti is produced principally from white Muscat grapes in the region of Piedmont. It makes a wonderful accompaniment to fresh fruit desserts, especially those flavoured with lemon or pear. Serve it very cold as an aperitif or after a meal.

...

PROSECCO

Prosecco is mainly the name of an old variety of grape from the Friuli region that is used to make a sparkling wine, or spumante, of the same name. It is fruity, simple and very pleasant, with a slight taste of almonds.

...

SAMBUCA

This anise- or licorice-flavoured liqueur is usually produced from star anise. Serve it plain, diluted with water or over ice before dinner, or in coffee after a meal. The Italian custom is to serve Sambuca in a little glass with three coffee beans and flambé it just before drinking.

...

MARTINI OR NOILLY PRAT VERMOUTH

Very similar in flavour, the former vermouth is Italian and the latter is French. Made from white wine to which herbs, spices and sugar have been added, these aperitifs are often used to make sauces. If you don't have any on hand, replace it with dry white wine.

...

VINO SANTO

Originating in Tuscany, this wine features notes of candied fruit, honey, hazelnut, caramel or praline, thanks to the production process, which involves drying the grapes in the sun to increase the concentration of sugar. A sweet wine, vino santo is sometimes referred to as the "nectar of the gods."

Grazie

THANKS To my mother, my father, my grandmother Laurence; in fact, my whole family! I owe you for the pleasure that sharing and cooking bring me. + To Stéphan Boucher, my wonderful accomplice. + To Jean Longpré, for the magnificent light in your photos, and to Nathalie, too, for your assistance. + To the team at orangetango – Mario, Élise, Isabelle – for the orange and the tango, your freshness and your colour. + To Monic Richard, for the precision of your gaze, and to Maxime, her assistant. + To Chantal Canse, André Perras and Colette Brossoit, my designated tasters, and to all the other willing mouths, for the generosity of your comments. + To Marie-Claude Goodwin, for being a good listener. + To Patrick Leimgruber, for your witty availability. + To Zone3 and Télé-Québec, for your confidence. + To the Italian Chamber of Commerce in Montreal, *grazie mille*. + To Josée Robitaille, for reading so carefully. + To Louise Pesant, for helping organize the book. + To Maryse Cantin: Thank you. + To Elena Faita, Steve, Jean-François and André: Thank you and thank you again. + To Anne Filion, for your enthusiasm. + To Gaz Métro, for your renewed support. + To everyone who shared their friendship and, at times, culinary expertise for this book. + To all the markets and artisanal producers whose high-quality products make all the difference. + And to all of you, who make me happy by reading my words.

ACCESSORIES For having helped us set the table so beautifully, thank you to Arthur Quentin + Atelier François Béraud (black steel table) + Couleurs + La Maison d'Émilie + Le temps des cigales (woodworking) + Les Touilleurs + Maison La Cornue + Moutarde + Quincaillerie Dante + Tom Littledeer (wooden utensils).

INDEX

A TAVOLA!

(Dinner's ready!)